Praise for 9

"Lucy Turner has produced a remarkable book of interest and charm. She has highlighted uplifting phrases from the many cultures she has worked among - and opens our eyes and minds to some memorable insights on life."
— Lord Robertson of Port Ellen,
10th Secretary General of NATO

"There is truth and joy in Lucy's perspective, and the world needs what she provides here, more than ever."
— Teresa Jennings, Vice President & Treasurer at LexisNexis Rule of Law Foundation

"An inspiring, focussed read about languages, life, story-telling, hope and a genuine, resourceful humanity. . . Writing from Scotland, we would say that *9 Wonder Words* is a *kist o riches* - a treasure chest of insights and experiences. That this is a *dram* of a book - a pick-me-up for struggling humans. That it is a *minding* in its thoughtful reflections and its earnest or promise of coping. That it is a *handsel* - a gift freely given with an inexhaustible potential to be freely handed onwards; *a makar's wark* - something made or crafted by a storyteller and poet, giving creative delight as well as wisdom. This truly a book to be savoured and shared round, a bit like Robert Burns' *cup of kindness for auld lang syne*."
— Donald Smith, Director,
Traditional Arts and Culture Scotland

"Breezy, lighthearted, and easy-to-read writing with a significant message. I smiled as I read it."
— Dr. Pauline Amos, artist and filmmaker

"A must-read to find joy in the world and an easy-to-read book for anyone."
— Deep Shikha, Professor of Economics,
St. Catherine's University

"I couldn't put it down. It resonated with so much of my own experience and articulated it better!"
— Alan Miller, Professor of Practice in Human
Rights Law

"A page-turner that opens your mind and repairs your perspective on life."
— Kevin Greer, artist

"A prescription for how to derive joy and purpose from doing your part to make the world better."
— T. Abate, via. LinkedIn.com

9
WONDER
WORDS

9 WONDER WORDS

A Language for Living Well—
Even When All Hell Breaks Loose

LUCY TURNER

ISBN: 978-1-7348400-8-7 (paperback)
ISBN: 978-1-7348400-3-2 (ebook)
ISBN: 978-1-7348400-2-5 (audiobook)

Library of Congress Cataloging-in-Publication Registration 2020926030

First Edition

Book design by Mayfly Design
Logo design by Andrew DiGenova

WOR(L)D

New York, NY
www.lucyturner.org

Proceeds from this publication go to:
The Welcoming and to the Scottish Storytelling Forum.
See https://www.thewelcoming.org
See https://www.storytellingforum.co.uk

To Mum and Dad
All of these stories are for you, and because of you.

Contents

Introduction

As an international civil servant at the United Nations Headquarters in New York City after more than ten years in Africa, Asia, the Middle East, and the Pacific, I discovered three things I will share with you in *9 Wonder Words: A Language for Living Well— Even When All Hell Breaks Loose*.

First, well I'll be damned! Living in places ravaged by war, poverty, tyranny, discrimination, division, and disease can be tough. Twenty hours a day without electricity or heating in the Himalayas. Shivering under yak wool blankets at -37 degrees in a home with no insulation. Dining by candlelight on dried fruit and nuts riddled with curious-looking holes. Sweating out a heat wave with no air conditioning. Lying restless in a bed full of bugs that bit me as rodents scuttled around it. "Bathing" for weeks with the soap-dabbed edge of a towel dipped in a bucket containing an inch of water. Commuting by convoy through streets lined by soldiers and protesters. Rescheduling assignments because my accommodation was bombed out of existence while I was en route. Malaria, typhoid, and a mystery parasite that left my skeletal body contorted in excruciating pain in the dead of night as monsoon rains hammered hot red earth—yes, my field work with the UN has not been as glamorous as my Mum made it out to be at ladies' lunches—though I'm glad she got a kick out of it.

Second, learning foreign languages makes life easier. I did it partly out of respect, and partly to get from A to B and pick up some oranges on the way. And it worked. I got home, I got snacks, and I learned cute ways to say, "I'm not going anywhere, sunshine—see you tomorrow!" to hecklers yelling, "White girl! Go home!" as I was on my way to work.

I also got answers to my many questions:

Why do people here yell so much?

Why do motorists push pedestrians off the road?

Why is there a live crocodile in this office?

These folks haven't eaten for two days, and woke up with sewage on their sheets: why are they smiling so much?

How come there is light in the slum when there is no generator or fuel or power in the grid?

Why is this clearly very poor woman I've never met before giving me sweet, warm, soft bread from a hole in the ground?

These folks sleep on a bench at the side of the road, breathe polluted air, drink dirty water, and eat no more than a few bites of food every few days—why are they talking about how grateful they are and saying, "*Ah di do jis fayn tenki, no get no problem*"? (I'm doing just fine, thank you, I don't have any problems.)

Me? I can see plenty of problems with this situation.

Until . . .

Until, through specific words, I gained access to different perspectives; perspectives through which I could look at the same scene and agree, "*No get no problem.*"

I was in more stressful, chaotic, and unpleasant environments than ever; feeling more relaxed, peaceful, and happier than ever. That was how learning local languages truly made my life easier, because I acquired words that served as "medicine for the mind." Their effect was to ease my irritation over . . . oh, everything, and enable me to notice and enjoy new forms of beauty and pleasure. This gave me new strength, and the ability to do more, achieve more, and enjoy more—no matter how challenging the situation may seem to be. Without yet knowing it, I had acquired a gift: a newfound resilience and ability to access an inner reserve of peace and strength.

My first steps back into the world of soft toilet paper and functioning plumbing systems was the security line at Heathrow airport, where people were having a meltdown about the waiting time. After witnessing plenty more first-world problems, such as, "Oh no, they've sold out of blueberry flaxseed muffins!!," I, who also love those muffins, realized that other people could benefit from the resilience I had acquired through language.

Third, language changes the way people think, see, act, and behave. A few years later, at UN headquarters in New York City, I found an unexpected benefit of being identified as the "native speaker" who must therefore do writing tasks for the team alongside my main job. Since the business of bureaucracy is largely based on writing (briefing notes, speeches, reports, letters, code cables, invitations, and such) there was plenty of this additional work. With *"Tell God, tenki, no get no problem"* (Tell God, thank you, I don't have any problems) and *"alhamdulillah"* (Thank God; thank God for this problem because a good thing will come of it) buzzing through my brain, I didn't complain. And sure enough, I discovered an unexpected blessing in the "burden" of being the team writer, a new understanding of the power of language.

To write and to speak is to put ideas in people's minds, introduce new thoughts to their brains, add new perspectives to their worldview. And if the writing is concise enough (single words, short phrases) and sufficiently compelling (human stories, statistics) people are led to not only understand but to care about those new ideas, possibilities, and their own power to create change. As colleagues in other agencies (who honestly had not always been very excited to work together) began to behave and express themselves in a slightly different way that suggested an appreciation of the ideas presented to them in speeches and reports, briefing notes, and code cables, I realized that maybe words could be more than just "medicine for the mind." Perhaps they could even be medicine for our world, and the institutions that serve it.

Huh?! But we need projects and programs, laws and policies, evidence-based formulas and formal interventions to create meaningful change, not mere sounds and scribbles!

Knowing this, still, my curiosity led me to look into the data and discover this one final thing about language: the idea that words can change the way we see, think, feel, act, and respond to other people and situations is proven in countless studies from numerous prestigious institutions. And of course, the mantra-chanting monks, speech-making politicians, and keyword-spinning marketing gurus knew this all along. You and I may not all be scientists, spiritually enlightened, or elected to public office, but we like to know about what works to make life better. I wrote this book for us.

9 *Wonder Words* is a way for me to share the gifts of a life of languages. I grew up in a family in which three were

spoken: English, Welsh, and Gaelic. I learned four more at school (Latin, French, Russian, and Italian) before learning countless more in a career spanning thirteen years and five continents, so far.

I wrote *9 Wonder Words* to help protect the rapidly depleting collective wisdom of humanity, held in more than 7,000 languages. I wrote it to help us adapt to diversity through words that promote intercultural understanding and appreciation. I wrote it because people's self-worth is so often bound to the respect accorded to their language; and by honoring diverse languages, we honor diverse peoples. Most of all, I wrote it to make people smile—and give them tools to keep smiling after they have closed the cover to crack on with Tuesday.

At the United Nations, I find ways for people affected by conflict and poverty to communicate with decision-makers, so they can get the resources and respect they need to flourish. In Liberia, Sierra Leone, Timor Leste, Nepal, Palestine, San Quentin State Prison, and now at HQ, I have seen how helping people speak and be heard promotes peace, empowerment, empathy, and measurable improvements in their lives and institutions.

The following chapters present some words of wisdom and wellness from languages around the world, which I discovered in places I visited and became immersed in for a time. I'm delighted to share them with you. Thank you.

1

Parole

> **Parole** (noun, feminine)
>
> **Pronunciation**: paʀɔl (pah-rohl)
>
> **Origin**: French. Derived from Latin *parabola* meaning "speech, discourse"; late fifteenth century from Old French for "word" or "formal promise."
>
> **Definition**: Word; music; lyrics. Common usage: *avoir la parole* (to have the floor); *donner la parole à quelqun* (give the floor to someone; to 'hand over'); *prendre la parole* (to speak).

How to use *parole, la parole*

You matter immensely, and so does everyone else. This is the observation written into international law, policy, and indeed, the entire international system. What you think matters. What you want matters. What you need matters. And it matters that you speak it. While people with great intuition, intelligence, empathy, and kindness could probably guess and give you everything you need all the days of your life, let's face it: you're not going to be surrounded by them every day. So to get to where you want to be, you'll need to use what French people call *la parole*: speak up; speak out; use your voice to make your needs and desires, demands, and perspectives known.

Take women for example: encouraged throughout history to be seen and not heard, they have relied on people around them to have crystal balls and generous spirits. That hasn't gone so well: the International Labour Organisation found that women are paid 20 percent less than men for the same work. Research from Carnegie Mellon University suggests that this gap exists simply because women typically do not use *la parole* to get what they want, need, and deserve: women are unlikely to ask for a raise (four times less likely than men), and when they do, women request 30 percent less than men do. Just 12.5 percent of women negotiate for their starting salary, compared to 52 percent of men. That leads to as much as $1.5 million in lost income over a woman's career. It's no surprise then that women are poorer than the other half of the human race. UN Women, a United Nations entity dedicated to gender equality and the empowerment of women, found that women and girls around the world are up to 24 percent more likely than men and boys to live in extreme poverty; 10 percent more likely to suffer from undernourishment; and more than 50 percent more likely to lack access to primary school education.[1] Data shows that COVID-19 hit "feminized" sectors of the economy hardest (health, education, and community services), leading to more women than men losing jobs and income, exacerbating these inequalities.

---

1. "Turning promises into action: Gender equality in the 2030 Agenda for Sustainable Development." UN Women (New York, 2018). https://www.unwomen.org/en/digital-library/publications/2018/2/gender-equality-in-the-2030-agenda-for-sustainable-development-2018

9 Wonder Words

Indigenous people often do not have *la parole* because they are not fluent in the official languages in which services are provided—from health and education to justice and security. And they often lack the opportunity to speak and be heard by decision-makers: a platform where they can articulate their concerns and demand accountability for effective responses to their needs. According to United Nations data, even though indigenous people make up 5 percent of the world's population, they account for more than 15 percent of the world's poorest, and lag behind on virtually every indicator of social, economic, and political progress.[2] So there we have it: those who cannot speak and be heard—those who do not have what the French call *la parole*—are those who suffer most.

What are we going to do? Sit down at the river and cry? Nope. We're going to build a bridge to the lives and world we want, one spoken word at a time.

The story in these statistics is an empowering one: if you can speak out, even if your voice shakes, then you can soar up beyond your present limitations, to a place that's closer to where you want to be. As you rise, you'll help others to rise up, too: we all benefit from your knowledge, experience, and talents.

So use *la parole* as a reminder of the power you possess somewhere around your throat area. Use it to say what you have in your head and your heart, to help you get what you want. And what you want? Like every other part of you: it matters.

---

2. "State of the World's Indigenous People," Secretariat of the Permanent Forum on Indigenous Issues, (New York, 2009). https://www.un.org/esa/socdev/unpfii/documents/SOWIP/en/SOWIP_web.pdf

How I discovered *la parole*

This is how I remember my childhood in rural Scotland: cartwheeling across the lawn, palms pressed into the hard tops of daisies, head-over-feet-over-head-over-feet. Dizzy, giggling, weaving back to brother and sister and pals who squeezed through the hedge to play and eat party rings and jig about to Jive Bunny Jukebox on the ghetto blaster—red plastic, full blast—or sledge through the snow in blue and yellow padded onesies. Making mud pies under the trees at the bottom of the garden; running in for a can of Mum's hair mousse to ice our creations. Twenty pence on a Friday for sherbet lemons and foam shrimps and chocolate buttons studded with sugar sprinkles, all in a white paper bag with a red Twizzler sticking out the top. Bundles of flowers—blossoms blooming all over our conservation village—except for the year we made perfume. "Perfume" that smelled of boiled vegetables and brought the police to our door, while we hid in the tortoise-shaped sandpit, green plastic shell pulled over up our heads. *It wisnae me!*

Summer was fishing odd creatures from rock pools to place in a bucket over the handlebars and bicycle home for cheese toasties and maybe an ice-cream with raspberry ripple sauce. Light until late—pink skies, orange crème-puff clouds—then a moon like a giant silver coin over the loch, jumping fish sparkling in its light.

Winter was *guising*—performing poetry or plays for neighbors while dressed as something ghoulish—and visits from a Grandpa who looks like Popeye, smokes like Popeye, sails like Popeye, and ties us up tight in a beach towel to swing around his head like a helicopter propeller.

Life was a bit different in England. Not all rosy and homey and kind. It didn't help, I suppose, that we moved during some sort of "storm of the century"—all windscreen-shattering icicles and broken heating systems; high winds, heavy rains and (unrelated, but coincident), a housing market melt-down that left our family homeless in a hotel and hoping for the best.

I tramped to school through snow so thick that it swallowed a good part of my six-year-old self. At regular intervals, gloved hands hooked under my armpits and hoisted me out of whatever ditch or pothole I slipped into.

With all that cold, I suppose you could understand folk being a bit frosty, and my efforts to make friends were utterly fruitless:

"Dja want a bit o ma jeelie piece?"

"Can ah get a wee shot on the swing?"

Noses twisted. Mouths turned down. Nope. No one wanted to share my jam sandwich. No one wanted to let me use the swings. No one wanted to get to know me at all:

"What dyoo talk like vat? What's wrong wiv ya? You sahnd stupid you do. Eye ate Scottish peepul."

There it was. The bleak mid-winter of 1990 was when I learned there is a politics of language: how you speak influences whether you belong, and the opportunities available to you. It doesn't matter what you have to say. It's possible that no one will even hear it, just because of how you sound when you say it. Just because it's a bit different. Worse. Inferior.

Not the lesson I hoped for, but a valuable one nonetheless for the woman I would become: an international civil servant working in countries brought to their knees by these dynamics—exclusion, discrimination, inequality—and the conflicts to which they lead.

But for now, I am only *wee*; a small child pained and puzzled by my peers. "*Hmmm* . . . . Well this isn't good. How am I going to fit in? How am I going to get on? I'm only six!"

I decided that there was only one thing for it: to try to fit in by talking like them.

Trying to fit in at school didn't go down well at home. When my Mum picked me up from school, I got in the back of the car—a red Nissan Sunny cut-and-shut from Castlemilk—with my new accent. She was not amused.

Turning around from the driver's seat, glowering, my mother said in Welsh: "What's wrong with you then? Why the hell are you talking like that Lewsi *fach*? Ey, you better stop that now before your father gets home, or there'll be ructions!"

So that was me then: one child, two accents.

An older child, or a more courageous one, might have battered through primary school, lonely but defiant in defense of their place of origin and place in the world. Me? I was not that child. I wanted to belong. To be included. To have the same opportunities as everyone else. The small comfort of a *wee pal* to share *ma jeelie piece*, and *tae get a wee shot on the swings* at break time. I wanted the chance to speak and be heard—even if I had different things to say or a different way to say them.

And that moment, freezing and friendless in a foreign place, was when I decided: as for me, in my life, I will let people speak and be heard. In their own voices, and in their own languages. A moment of political awakening at the age of six, jam sandwich in hand, standing under the monkey bars in a padded onesie.

I once lived next door to an epigeneticist. Fascinating stuff. Turns out that we are made of lots of things—not only our own experiences and Mum and Dad's genes, but also Granny and Grandpa's. Yes, research exploring the intergenerational effects of trauma shows that our ancestors' experiences of hardship and violence can leave their mark on us too, through mutations in the genetic code itself. Events in our predecessors' lives can change the way their DNA is expressed, and that change can pass to the next generation.

So next time you have a "gloves off" reaction over Sunday brunch which surprises everyone—"Whoa!!?! I only said that the pancakes taste a bit different today!"—maybe a brow-beaten *babushka* in your lineage had something to do with it. And maybe my visceral reaction to exclusion—silencing, shaming, enforced conformity, and all the other indignities and implications of deprivation of the right to speak and be heard—came from somewhere and someone else.

Both of my parents' languages (Gaelic, Welsh) were suppressed. Their usage banned, their speakers shamed, as a way to consolidate English control over Scotland and Wales. You can see the logic: a person's culture is often their source of strength, belonging, wisdom, and confidence. So if you wanted to (not that you would, of course; lovely you); but say if you wanted to diminish resistance to your plans for someone, it would seem to be a good idea to stop them using the language that transmits their culture and resilience. That is why the banning of language has happened throughout history, and is still happening. The more common approach is simply to discriminate against speakers of a minority language (such as by not providing them with services) and allow the language to die out as people stop using and sharing it. Either way, *linguicide* (death of language) is a thing, and so too its effects on people around the world.

Well, I don't want to bum you out, but there it is: *linguicide*. I've had no big moral mission to end it, nor to assert language rights. The focus of my work has been different: helping to promote justice and security. But I decided that in anything I did for this job (writing a report, designing a project, drafting a brief, preparing a video, or what have you), I would try to enable as many people as possible to speak and be heard. I would, as the French say, try to give *la parole* (the floor; the opportunity to speak and be heard) to people who didn't usually have it. I thought that if I could put the people who were usually silent in policy-making discussions, and invisible to decision-makers, into my work—using as often as possible their actual voices and phrasing when I couldn't get them in a room with those authorities—then maybe I could offer them *la parole*.

So the nuts and bolts of my professional life were simple. I talked to people. That's it. I talked to people who couldn't speak the main national language(s), people in remote areas, uneducated people, people who weren't normally consulted; and fed their words into whatever I did in support of national authorities.

I did it on principle, for that tiny tot in the playground, and perhaps for a silenced and shamed relative who passed their altered gene expression off to me (Thanks, Grandma!).

But I tell you, it was the most practically useful thing I could have done—besides, say, learning how to mend toilets and make a candle out of molten bits of wax and wick. Because (you heard it here first!) when you ask people things, they tell you things. And when you enable them to speak in their own voices and languages, they tell you even more things. Things that you don't know—things that would never even have occurred to you. Things that reveal them to be real experts—not in commodity trading or quantum electrodynamics perhaps—but in their own lives. Experts on their own needs, their own desires, their own experiences, lived in their own families, homes, communities, and the institutions in which they work or interact.

That practical knowledge, that everyday expertise, was the information I needed to do my job. Sure, I had my own knowledge from years of study and work. But what I learned from the people to whom I spoke was almost always more interesting, impactful, and innovative than what I already knew, and more useful than what I thought.

Take Palestine, for example, where a large United Nations program aimed to help marginalized people access life-improving entitlements like pensions, inheritance, or convictions for crimes committed against them. We did a nationwide public perception survey to inform the next phase of the program.

What can I tell you? The survey showed that the justice system was only really serving relatively wealthy, well-educated, urban males. The disadvantaged people targeted by the UN program (women, indigenous people, those with low-income, limited education, and living in remote areas) were not even *trying* to access it. And what the program was doing to change this—sensible things suggested by Palestinian justice sector professionals (prosecutors, judges, lawyers) and their advisors like scrapping court fees and providing free legal representation and training on judgment writing—were not the right things. They addressed the *assumed*, not the *actual*, reasons why people weren't accessing justice. Money not as well invested as it could have been, decisions not as well made—and all because people did not have *la parole*. Peace and progress held back because people could not speak and be heard about what they thought, wanted, needed, and what could be done about it. The things that people consulted through the survey proposed were different to what experts expected and professionals suggested, like "confusion on where to go in court," "lack of toilets," and "dirty buildings." The program was adapted to include simple responses like signage and sanitation, and the second survey a few years later demonstrated significant improvements in access to justice.

Just before this triumph, a UN Special Envoy (based in Castlemilk, as it happens) convened a meeting to consider such information, and ways to improve lives in the occupied Palestinian territory (as it was then called). The meeting opened with the usual hand-wringing about the hopelessness of "the situation," followed by a thorough review of data on human rights abuses. A detailed consideration of institutional failures followed midmorning coffee. And a post-lunch slump brought a rundown of reasons for why trying to make life even just a little better for the poorest people was pointless. *Sigh*.

It was late in the afternoon. Energy was low after the last of the coffee had been pumped from the pot. The sun had fallen so deeply on the horizon that lights were turned on. Strip lights flickered, pupils constricted, eyes blinked—and watches, shaken down from shirt sleeves, were consulted to know just when this miserable meeting would end. Just then, a woman dressed in a black chiffon scarf and *abeya* stood up.

With a soft voice, she said these words: "Colleagues; shall we curse the darkness, or light a candle in it?"

And there it was.

When people have *la parole*, they'll say things. They'll say things that change the way problems are understood, solutions are seen, decisions are made, resources are invested, and support is provided. They'll say things—simple things; common-sense things; the practical knowledge of day-to-day lived experience; insightful, profound, wise things—that can change the course of a day, discussion, decision, investment, plan, policy, program, law, and as many lives as people that hear it. Things until that moment unknown, unimagined, until those words conjure the idea in the mind of the person that hears it. They'll say things to make you laugh—and sometimes even to roll your eyes ("Well now you see the reason we don't have too many female lawyers in this country is because they would get tired climbing the steps to court")—but at least help you understand why we are where we are, and how to get somewhere else. When people have *la parole*, they say things to surprise, inspire, inform, uplift, encourage, amaze. They say things that make change happen.

"They" includes you, my dear. You, that beautiful Palestinian lady standing in the dim room in Jerusalem, and me.

I was going to write "ordinary" people, but I know that you and I are not ordinary. Our experiences are totally unique. Totally unique in all of human history. Your genes, the particular social, cultural, economic, and political context in which you were raised, the specific experiences you have had, are totally unique. And so, my dear reader, there's only been one of you in all of history. There will only ever be one of you in all of history. And if you don't say what you know to be true, if you don't express how you see things, or what you think, need, want to be able to realize whatever you observe to be important, for you, and for others, then it is lost. It is lost for all of us, forever.

There's a particular pen I like so very much. I wrote everything in these pages and more with it; in rapture since I discovered it almost a year before. But it just ran out of ink. With the pandemic not yet over, and all still shut, I'd have to search online to order some more. In the meantime, I'm writing with another pen I fished out of an old cardboard box with pens and paperclips and Post-it notes and the odd USB stick and stack of staples. It's a pen from my stint the previous summer at the Harvard Graduate School of Education. The university's motto is written on the shaft: *veritas* (truth). The motto of Harvard University used to be *Christo et Ecclesiae*— for Christ and Church—but they changed it to "Truth." Fair enough. God, Church, Truth—and for that matter, beauty, love, hope, joy—all aim to underpin the same thing: peace, progress, and the happiness to which they lead. Throughout history, priests, professors, and professionals with specific expertise have been regarded as the principal sources of that truth: the architects of an ever-better world. And there is a place for them—an important place, of course, for all learned people.

There is also a place for you and me. For you and me, and the UN Special Envoy, and that Palestinian lady, and everyone else. There is a place for what we know to be true; for our different perspectives, born of our unique experiences. There is a need for our knowledge. And there is a need for us to speak it. We must have *la parole*, so that others may benefit from what we know—and we can be seen, supported, recognized, respected, appreciated, valued, compensated in the way that we deserve.

I don't want to put you to work. I'd like to tell you that it's fine—just relax and take it easy, because it's all taken care of. Human rights exist, universally agreed by all of the world's governments ("Crack open the champagne!"). The idea that all people, including you and me, have an inherent "dignity and worth" that makes us automatically deserving of those equal rights, and able to contribute to "social progress and better standards of life in larger freedom," is old news. Old, old news. Nothing to see here. It's all been taken care of, so fret not, friend! Just go right ahead and enjoy your better standards of life in larger freedom—"Cheers!" *Clink!*

But I can't.

I can't because in a career trying to understand and influence power in favor of people who don't have it, you learn a thing or three about how it works. Not about the "dignity and worth" bit. Your dignity and worth, and the idea that it makes it possible for you—yes, little old you! mighty and magnificent you!—to make a unique contribution to all of humanity and human history was put forward by the ancient Greeks. Yes, big hitters like Socrates and Plato and Aristotle saw you coming, and what they had to say about you has never been successfully disputed since. No one's really learned anything more about that that isn't a confirmation of your importance since at least 470 BC.

But like I say, in more than a decade "popping the hood" of poverty to dig around the engine room of disempowerment, I discovered there's a caveat. Or perhaps I should say a key—a key to unlocking that potential within you, a key to accessing the wisdom and capability that lies under your skin and your doubts, making it possible for you to achieve whatever vision you have for yourself. Find and use that key, and you can enjoy making an important contribution to the economic, social, and cultural wealth of the whole world—and all of history, no less. Yes, exactly! It really is a jumping-up-and-down, eye-gogglingly immense prospect. Fireworks and bangers—behold! The beauty of you!

But let's not get carried away, because there are no guarantees that we will do it. No guarantees at all that we will do anything worthy of those sparklers. First, we must find the key. And we must use it to unlock that potential within us. A potential that Eleanor Roosevelt and all the world's governments called an "inherent dignity and worth," the Ancient Greeks called *entelechy,* and the Islamic, Jewish, Christian, Sikh, and Hindu scriptures refer to as a light or a candle. Which is exciting! Can you imagine?! Within you—little old you! mighty and magnificent you!—a vibrant light that can illuminate the path to a better life, a flame that can burn away the obstacles to a better world.

Yes, but like I said, let's curb our enthusiasm here because there are no guarantees that we'll do it. First, we need that key. Without it, we're just glimpsing on tip toes at this beautiful vision of a better life and world from behind a very thick door with a tiny window at the top.

Give me just one minute please of your precious time, and I'll show you the key I found in the rubble and resilience of conflict-affected countries on four continents—with no risk to you of malaria, and no need for a yellow fever certificate. Sound good?

Well alright then—let's do this together.

Who are the powerful? The powerful are those who can speak and be heard: who can speak the language of power; have a vote; a seat at the table; a space on the agenda; a buddy in the editorial department of the national newspaper; a big marketing team to influence public policy, national spending, and social norms to suit them. The powerful are the "squeaky wheels" who get the grease. The powerful are those who can speak and be heard.

Who are the powerless? The powerless are the disenfranchised minorities who cannot speak official languages; the uneducated people who cannot use them well. The indigenous peoples banned from speaking their mother tongue. The detainees behind thick prison walls. The environment, which has no voice. The women and children who "should be seen and not heard," and all those who "suffer in silence."

Who has changed their life, and the world? Those who change their own lives, and the lives of others, are those who speak out—even if what they have to say is uncomfortable to say, or inconvenient to hear.

And who are you? So many questions, and really just one: who has *la parole*? Who can speak and be heard?

And this is the key, my dear: *la parole*.

La parole is the way that your value—what you know, what you think, what you can do, and what you need to be able to do it—become known, and you can be appreciated, compensated, and situated in a context where you can thrive.

It would be nice obviously, if you could just get it all anyway; get all the support you need while swinging on a hammock and sipping on a piña colada. It would also be nice probably to have kombucha on tap in your kitchen, Italian mountain spring water streaming from your shower head, peace on earth, and goodwill to all men.

But we don't live in that world. As things stand, you'll more likely get the rights you deserve IF you speak out. You'll make the contribution of which you are capable IF you use your voice. You'll get the life you want and help create the future we need IF you use the power of *la parole*.

La parole is the reason this book exists; as an expression of my belief that every voice must be heard. We've got a few problems—you don't need me to list them, like some compliments list for the devil—and as Einstein said, "We cannot solve our problems with the same thinking we used when we created them."

The fresh thinking we need is all over our earth, in the many voices and languages of (extra)ordinary people who live in unique conditions—including those who have been silenced and silent, shamed and ashamed, censored and self-censoring. This book is another attempt to help to give them *la parole*, and enable the rest of us to benefit from what they have to say, by collecting together specific words they use to express their knowledge.

But that's not important right now. The important thing right now is YOU are here. The answers we all need also lie within you: in what you know, what you think, what you want, and what you need to be able to do it. What you know matters immensely—because you matter immensely—and it matters that you speak it. This is the key to getting the world we want and the future we need.

So forget "the world" for a moment. Right here and now, there is no "world." There is you and me and these words written for you. For YOU to use the power of your voice FOR YOU. FOR YOU to get the level of respect and recognition, space and support, confidence and compensation which you deserve, and which you will get by speaking out. There is a link between speaking out and soaring up, and that's what I want for you. To reach for the stars because why not? Isn't it your time now? Don't you deserve it? Don't the people who will benefit from your thriving deserve it? And aren't all the indications that everything is shifting now (necessity being the mother of all inventions) to make new things possible for you, as a person empowered with *la parole*?

So here it is. *La parole* is an invitation for you to speak up, no matter what accent you have or what language you use. Speak up, knowing that what you have to say, how you see things, and what you want is a jewel of inestimable value. As indeed, are you.

———

"At the end of each meeting, President Obama would ask anyone who had not already spoken what they thought. He would gain new and different insight from the women in particular. One day, in a meeting with just women, he prodded all of us to be more vocal. 'Speak up!,' he said. 'I need to hear from you.' It was then that I realized that if I didn't speak up, I wasn't just holding myself back—I wasn't doing my job." — Jennifer Palmieri.

2

Abracadabra

Abracadabra

Pronunciation: ə-ˈbra-kə ˈda-ˈbra (ab-rah-ka-da-bra)

Origin: Hebrew. Derived from Aramaic *avra kehdabra*; cabalistic or gnostic name for supreme god, word of power.

Definition: I create as I speak; it will be created with my words.

How to use *abracadabra*

Well, whaddaya know? Turns out that all those things you've been doing to be happy—pursuing promotions and prizes and pay raises and what have you—account for only 10 percent of your felt sense of happiness. Yes, that's all: 10 percent. According to groundbreaking research by happiness researcher Sonja Lyubomirsky, a more significant determinant of happiness is not what's in your world, but how you look at it.[3]

---

3. "Pursuing Happiness: The Architecture of Sustainable Change." *Review of General Psychology* Lybomirsky, Sheldon and Schkade, 2005. http://sonjalyubomirsky.com/wp-content/themes/sonjalyubomirsky/papers/LSS2005.pdf

What you notice, where you focus, how you interpret. In these lie the keys to happiness. That's why friends back from Sierra Leone or the Serengeti or Sahara say things like, "And do you know what's amazing, Maureen? They had nothing at all, but they were so happy!"

It's also why well-meaning people tell you to THINK POSITIVE! IT'LL MAKE EVERYTHING BETTER! And maybe it will. Except now you feel worse, because on top of all the other nonsense today, this: the insinuation that feeling bad is all your fault. Punishment somehow, for not looking on the bright side of life.

Fret not, friend! There are no positivity police in these pages. Only this: help to become one of those people who have the ability (let's call it a gift) to see the roses among the thorns, help in the form of words that wire your brain for happiness. *Abracadabra* invites you to use words to become one of those people who notice the sunrise and the sunset, the small kindnesses and daily loveliness that coexist with cruelty and ugliness. Yes, words. Not words like "scaffolding" or "chickenpox." But words from places like Sierra Leone and the Sahara and the Serengeti. Single, specific words without a direct English translation, which can change the way you look at people, places, and situations. Foreign words that help you see the world in a way that reveals its beauty. Words of wisdom. Words of wellness. The words in this book.

You already know that words are powerful, no? The power of words is the reason politicians make speeches, marketing is a multi-billion-dollar industry, and monks chant. It's the reason why hate speech can land you in prison, why the voiceless are the powerless, and why words—on stages and scrolls, pages and pamphlets, books and billboards— shape our lives and societies. Churchill, Gandhi, Mandela, Wilberforce, Wollstonecraft, you and I; all of us are word magicians.

Word magic may even be the essence of our humanity. According to evolutionary biologists, our species *homo sapiens* actually came into existence when our neanderthal ancestors developed the gene for language (*FOXP2*). Other research shows that words rework us from the inside, literally rewiring our brains to change how we think, speak, act, and relate to other people and situations. Using words from different languages can change the way we see the world and interpret each other, creating the mental underpinnings of 90 percent of our happiness.

How about that then, eh? This all sounded so "woo-woo" and "out there" and "*hmm*, not sure I want to keep reading this" a moment ago, but then *abracadabra! alakazam!* word magic became word science. And now the scribes, story-tellers, and scientists agree with the wizards: words—mere puffs of air lighter than a feather, shapes scrawled with a quill, spells spoken with the flick of a wand—are a powerful creative force.

What about you? Do you think that the driving force of evolution, the capability that created our species, the tech-nology that made possible every step of our progress toward peace and prosperity in larger freedom, the creative capacity behind cathedrals and the Concorde, the internet and iPhone, can help you have a better day?

Worth a punt, I reckon.

How I discovered *abracadabra*

On the bedside table of my childhood bedroom was an illuminated globe. Part decoration, part lamp, part pedagogical tool, I loved it for its soothing blue glow, and for its stories.

I didn't have bedtime books, you see. Instead, I'd spin the globe, place my finger on any part of its surface to stop its revolutions, and my father (the latest in a long line of sailors) would tell a tale from his time in that place. Wonderful stories of pirates and piranhas and pool parties with sharks and sailors in grass skirts; bright white beaches stretching into the distance as far as the eye can see; sand so fine that it squeaked as you walked on it, so white that it glowed in the moonlight. I'd drift off to sleep soothed by these stories: tucked up in bed, loved and safe and well, almost hearing the sound of the sea washing the shore; feeling the breeze ruffling my hair, cooling, calming, as my feet sink into softened sand, and I squint under a sunhat, admiring the sky that is always there as the earth spins on its axis, oblivious to our triumphs and tribulations.

I sometimes long for those peaceful places. When world leaders threaten nuclear war over Twitter, rising sea levels threaten to sweep away coastal cities, and everyone seems to have become a racist or communist or bewildered bystander wondering, *What the hell?* Who can say it wouldn't be nice to get away from it all? Especially on "days like these"—the ones with a to-do list 2.5 A-4 pages long in 10-point print and the pinging of emails and the ponging of WhatsApp and BING! of texts and *BRRRRING!* of phone calls makes it impossible to actually get on with the things on the list, and construction in the next building is beginning to sound like they're actually drilling inside your skull damn! And the rent is due.

Mind frantic, then freezing in some sort of systems overload; rainbow pinwheel appearing behind your eyes, candy colors spinning as if to say, "I told you, you had too many windows open," and leaving only one half-coherent thought, *Stop the world; I want to get off!*

And so you daydream about your exciting future in which someone else answers your phone and does your laundry; watch videos of cats playing the piano and high-fiving a dog; and check out beach vacations before ending up at the coffee shop, clutching a latte and hoping for the best.

GOOD NEWS! You can reach gentler moments and peaceful places without going anywhere, taking anything, or spending anything at all.

Abracadabra!

A flash! A spark! A sputter. A plume of smoke. And then . . . nothing. You're still here, 6.45 p.m. and a new deadline just arrived in the inbox, due by 10:00 a.m. tomorrow. And let me check—ah yes, climate, social, political, economic crises all over the globe.

Ah well, don't be disheartened, this is part of the magic. *Abracadabra*, a Hebrew word meaning "I create as I speak," expresses the power of language to change the way you experience the circumstances in which you find yourself. With specific words and phrases, you can escape the stress of certain situations without actually leaving the ground on which you stand. Be in them, and be well. Specific words from foreign languages, most without a direct English translation, convey ideas that can reframe the way you see a situation, providing perspectives that help you to face them with strength and a sense of humor, and priming you to notice nice things that you might otherwise overlook.

A word is a form of attention, and some foreign words focus our attention in ways that make us happier: on the many forms of beauty around us, and the many good things for which we can be grateful.

Sound far-fetched? Fair enough. I probably wouldn't have believed it myself. But a lifetime of language learning taught me that the words we use—the ones we say to ourselves and to each other—can rewire our brains, shape our lives, and change our world. In a word, *abracadabra*: an ancient word with modern scientific underpinnings. Before I studied the research, I saw the reality: people and places changed by language. So how about we discover it together in the way I did: adventure before academia? Here—spin the globe why don't you? I'll tell you all about it.

Ah, Nepal: that lilting, lovely place nestled in the mighty Himalaya. It's a sleepy Sunday in spring, still early, pinkish light in the sky, and Kathmandu is quiet. Ladies in saris and cardigans, socks and sandals, waft incense, mouthing mantras over a brass plate. Others sweep dust onto the red earth road. Dogs move slowly, still waking up. Jacaranda trees bloom purple in the street; pink, orange, yellow, white, magenta bougainvillea spill over the high walls of gated and guarded residences. Blossoms unbound by convention, sharing their beauty with the well-to-do *Brahim* and the downtrodden *Dalit* alike. A floral "f- you!" to the caste system, set among the usual mix of the sacred and the profane. Huge piles of rubbish on the roadside, sacred statues and stupas. Chains of magnolia strung between temple walls over the Bagmati river, animal carcasses rotting in the water. Dreadlocked holy men with painted faces in orange *dhoti* and mala beads texting on an iPhone. Stray dogs, wandering cows, and an enormous elephant, twenty-feet tall at least, walking past the Human Rights Commission.

By the time I reach Boudhanath—the 38-meter-tall stupa in the Tibetan part of town—the city is more awake, as though roused with *chiya* to the noise of bike engines and car horns and squeaky parts in minibuses, ringing *tingsha* bells, murmured mantras, and yelling.

Every sound is silenced when I step into Namaste Bookshop: a peaceful place filled with the sweet scent of soap and candles, the soothing sound of Sanskrit singing, and the pleasing sight of lokta paper. Lots and lots of lokta paper. There are books in front, books behind; books to my left. And to my right, light pours in through large windows, soft light shining on singing bowls, *khukri* knives and several sizes of *dorje*: a mystical symbol that looks like . . . a formation of synchronized swimmers? A hat? Its meaning is revealed only to the enlightened; I have no idea. But you can probably Google it.

I get chatting to the owner, Surya ji. Heck, I get chatting to anyone. I am my mother's daughter, you see. And my mother, dear reader, gets chatting to e-v-e-r-y-o-n-e. I call her Mims. She's a Welsh-speaking, daffodil-wearing, rugby-loving lady from a little house in a valley surrounded by sheep. The house doubled as the village shop, giving tiny Mims (then known as Heather a'stores) liberal access to chats, sherbet lemons, and the ability to sell things. She's continued to seek out all of those things ever since (her cake stall at the annual Christian Aid Sale is a real money spinner). Mims has lived long enough outside West Wales to become more quiet and reserved, but what can I tell you? It didn't happen.

And because it didn't happen, Mims has a deep bench. She's always got someone who'll mend the doorbell or bring over some venison that was more than they could fit in the freezer, or a head of cauliflower that they couldn't get through before going on holiday, and know just the right person to help John down the road find a spare part for his vintage car. If I ever have an idea or partially formed desire for anything at all, she'll know someone that can help me with it; someone that she met while choosing tomatoes in Tesco, "which was funny, really, because I never go to Tesco." They say we're only six connections away from Gwyneth Paltrow. Not Mims! I wouldn't be surprised if she met GP's cousin at the bus stop last week, over for the festival and a little trip to Skye. My mum says things like, "Honest to God, you'd think Skye was the only place in Scotland outside Edinburgh! They all say 'and next week, we're going to Skye!' Apparently, people on Skye are getting so fed up of tourists."

This—in case you're wondering—is how I got to learn lots of languages, and write this book. I was exposed to a few at home (Gaelic, Welsh, English), and I learned a few more at school (Russian, French, Italian, Latin, Greek). But the real reason is that in every one of the five continents where I lived and worked over thirteen years at the United Nations, I was my mother's daughter. And so my mother's daughter got chatting to Surya ji about all manner of things: local writers and book binding, the weather and the load-shedding, food shortages and the constitutional crisis, and whose elephant was that wandering around Sanepa this morning?

"के गर्ने जीवन त्यस्तै हो" "*Kay garnay?*" के गर्ने I say, with the customary shrug of the shoulders. जीवन त्यस्तै हो *jindagi yestai ho.*" The Nepali phrase, almost as common as "Hello," was uttered on days when you couldn't get to work because of a *bandha* (strike), and you couldn't buy food beyond a few wrinkly tomatoes because of protests in the Terai. Or when you had to queue for five hours for gas because of a trade dispute with India, sitting in the street on your cylinder until the metal imprinted on your bum. Or when you're eating an omelet and *oh!* a monkey jumped on your head. In moments like this, saying *Kay garnay? Jindagi yestai ho?* is a way to stay cool when it's not clear how getting wound up will help.

Yes or no? In Southeast Asia, it's sometimes hard to know. Both are expressed by a bobbing of the head, so you have to look carefully to notice the exact angle, speed, and frequency the head bobs about on the shoulders. At this moment, the shaking head of this gentle, warm, and soft-spoken man is very clear: HELL NO! कुनै! तपाईंले त्यो भन्नु हुँदैन. *Kunai! Tapā'īnlē tyō bhannu huṁdaina!* We can-oooooot say things like that anymore! We must do something to change, nuh? We must create *Naya Nepal* नयाँ नेपाल (new Nepal). "And actually we are, isn't it so?"

Absolutely. The country was indeed changing dramatically and at an astonishing pace. Between 1990 and 2000, the country changed from absolute monarchy to multi-party democracy. From war to peace. From a unitary state to a decentralized, federal state. From a Hindu country to a secular country. From a winner-takes-all, majoritarian (first-past-the-post) electoral system to an inclusive, mixed system. And all in just a few years. All in—historically speaking—the blink of an eye.

I leave the shop with an armful of books and a headful of incoherent thoughts about the power, purpose, and potential of language. Could words really be creative? Might there be something to *matrika shakti*: the Hindu concept of the vibratory power of the word, and the myth of Brahma the creator as a golden egg of sound? Could it really be that a change in the whole political, social, and economic structure of the country was seeded in new ways of thinking, supported by a new way of speaking? Could these massive changes be underpinned by language? By rejecting "all in the hands of the gods" thinking, and the words that expressed it, for a new language of human rights in *Naya Nepal*? Which is to say, were Nepalis really creating a new reality by speaking it into existence?

Head spinning amid the sound and smell and sight of incense and burning ghee lamps, bells and spinning prayer wheels, sweets and spices and paints piled high, I was searching for something; some memory to make sense of the odd moment in the bookshop. Mind whirling, searching, I wandered with the devotees, shuffling around the stupa and into a dark doorway with giant prayer wheels. Still wondering what it was that I couldn't remember; some sense of a forgotten something. I spun the prayer wheels, one by one, red and gold metal spinning . . . spinning . . . spinning . . . turning endless revolutions . . . And as the red and gold of the metal turning, turning, turning, turning, turned to the red and gold sky of a West African sunset, I remembered. I remembered Sierra Leone.

A striking vision: young men whose limbs were amputated during one of the twenty-first century's most tragic wars playing football on the sand. No legs. Deftly moving the ball with crutches beneath a glorious orange sunset. Where there had once been the hacking of limbs and the burning of villages, mass rape and economic collapse, there was now this: hope, energy, enthusiasm for a better future, and the determination to create it. And underneath it all? A change in language.

How do I know? I lived there, I worked there, and I crunched the numbers.

Our project aimed to end impunity for human rights abuses by helping people to access justice. Part of my job involved collecting data on overall crime rates, number of crimes reported to police, number that go from police to prosecution, number that go from prosecution to the courts, number of judgments executed, etc.

The figures were miserable. Month after month, violence and poverty proliferated in a context of impunity, perpetuated by a sense of powerlessness reinforced in daily conversations. The poor people we were trying to help mostly would not hold perpetrators of violence accountable, or claim life-improving entitlements like trading licenses, education, or vaccination programs for themselves or their children. Many didn't know that they had rights; and most feared the stigma, cost, retribution, or time wasted trying to claw justice from weak institutions. The national language (*Krio*) reflected a sense of powerlessness and the inevitability of suffering in suboptimal circumstances. Even in the face of horrific violations, people would say:

"*Dis nar life*" (This is life).

"*Na fobiya, no mo*" (You just have to put up with it).

"*Man dey suffer*" (Life is suffering).

"*Ah no go able*" (I can't).

"*Man dey suffer, no to so?*" (People suffer, isn't it so?).

And so it was: Sierra Leone was the poorest country in the world, with little prospect of that sorry statistic changing any time soon.

I'm not sure how it happened, or when. There was no government effort or charity project or MC Saachi-style campaign. All I can tell you is this: zippy, upbeat new words and phrases entered Krio vocabulary:

"*Wan day, ee go betteh*" (Things will get better).

"*We go mek am!*" (We'll make it).

"*Man fo do sumtin fo isef*" (You've got to make the effort).

"*We go do am.*" (We'll do it!).

"*No to die God.*" (God isn't dead).

"*Saffol, saffol. Small, small.*" (Bit by bit, step by step).

It was an interesting and insignificant thing. Words: mere puffs of air and sounds in the streets. What of it?

This: as words changed, lives changed. You could see it, feel it. A change in attitude and sense of possibility. You could measure it: a 165 percent increase in prosecutions for gender-based violence in just one year.

Did the replacement of demotivating phrases by energizing words cause the change? I'm just saying it's interesting, isn't it? Interesting to observe the concomitant changes: one in the streets, one in my spreadsheets.

No more talk of spreadsheets. Let's spin again.

Heathrow airport.

My first steps back into the world of soft toilet paper and functioning plumbing systems was the security line at Heathrow, where folks were having a meltdown about wait times. Eyes popping, head shaking, fingers raked roughly through thinning hair, heavy sighs and the gnashing of teeth; the length of the queue appeared to be shortening lives.

"What's happening here?!"

"Why don't they put more people on duty?!"

"Can't they see there are hundreds of us?!"

"How long have we been waiting here, Jack?"

"When I get to the desk, I'm going to give them a piece of my mind."

"Yeah, you tell 'em!"

Surveying the scene, I stifled a grin. What on earth? Why are they flipping out over such a small thing?

Hang on . . . Why am I *NOT* flipping out over this small thing?

Not naturally either patient or relaxed, I could see there, right there standing in line at airport security, both who I had been, and who I had become. Who had I been? Well you'd have to ask my mum, but I'm just going to go with "a pain in the ass," probably. Irritated about the shop running out of flaxseed muffins ("but I love those muffins!"). Annoyed about bathing with the soap-dabbed edge of a towel dipped in a bucket. Frustrated by the bedbugs that bit me, and the slightest delay, and the perpetually broken toilet and every time someone didn't meet my standards (including me). Confused by, oh, everything really. Why do people here yell so much? Why do motorists push pedestrians off the road? These folks haven't eaten for two days, and woke up with sewage on their sheets: why are they smiling all the time? Why is this clearly very poor woman I've never met before giving me sweet, warm, soft bread from a hole in the ground? Delicious but still . . . This couple that sleeps on a bench at the side of the road, breathes polluted air, drinks dirty water, and eats no more than a few bites of food every few days—why are they talking about how grateful they are and saying, "*Ah di do jis fayn tenki, no get no problem*" (I'm doing just fine thank you, I don't have any problems).

Me? I could see plenty of problems with this situation. But here I was, standing in line at security, observing a scene of some frustration and agreeing: "No get no problem."

A jazz review I once read said, "It was strange. They played really slow, and then really fast."

And that was how it happened.

I had noticed for a while that specific foreign words and phrases frequently came to my mind. Some because they are efficient: a single word for something that would require many English words. Others changed the way I see: they describe an aspect of the world's beauty, and draw attention to an otherwise unnoticed loveliness.

Some help to understand people from different countries and cultures. Others describe ideas and innovations to address social and environmental challenges. Some are comforting. Some are funny. Others support sanity by shifting perspectives on stressful situations—like the Arabic *alhamdulillah* (gratitude in anticipation of a benefit to derive even from undesirable situations); the Tibetan *drala* (a spirit that emerges when you resolve to do something, to give you the power to achieve it, even in the most impossible circumstances); and all those upbeat *Krio* phrases that Sierra Leoneans spoke while smiling, starving, and sick in a slum, or struggling to squeeze justice from a broken system.

Fresh off the car-boat-bus-plane from Freetown, these (latter) words came to mind as I stood in the crowd of red eyes and inflatable neck pillows. As they went round around in a multilingual mental loop, I wondered:

Could words lie between who I had been, and who I had become?

Could words really create change?

Could there be some sort of magical power of language? Some powerful effect of mere puffs of air, mixed with sound and vibration?

Ah . . . probably not.

But . . . maybe?!

But probably not. Yeah, probably not.

So I went through the security gates—and more, and more all over our green and lovely earth, for years—until cartwheels! backflips! A victory lap of high fives! Home.

Home to Scotland. Home to running water. Home to heating, electricity, political stability, ordered traffic, scones, tea, tea cakes, tea breaks, and windows without bars. Home to spare time. Yes, with no toilets to repair, or water to carry, or gas to install, or rats to chase, I had time to explore The Language Thing. And this is what I found: I'm not the only one. It turns out that my lived experience of a mind and life changed by language is the subject of hundreds of millions of dollars of research in the world's finest academic institutions.

For months, I read research from the fields of linguistics, cognitive psychology, positive psychology, evolutionary biology, and neuroscience, to find the answer to a question I once asked while standing in line at Heathrow airport: can the difference between two people who look at a scene—one set on fire with rage; one feeling fine—be linked to language?

Well, strap yourself in because—*abracadabra! alakazam!* It turns out that yes indeed:

Language influences our perceptions. Some languages, like Greek, have two words for blue (*ghalazio* for light blue, and *ble* for a darker shade). A study found that Greek speakers could discriminate between shades of blue faster and better than native English speakers. Studies also show that speakers of languages that attribute genders to objects (like in French *une table* or *un pont*) associate those objects with masculine and feminine properties respectively. They describe the table as elegant or beautiful, and the bridge as strong, or durable.

Language changes the physical structure of the brain. Studies show that language learning strengthens the nerve fibers that carry information to various parts of the brain, strengthening the prefrontal cortex (the part of the brain involved in organizing information, planning, reasoning, and working memory). This is why bilingual people, on average, are diagnosed with dementia 4.5 years later than monolinguals.

Language influences how we see other people. When Arabic-Hebrew bilinguals were asked to match Arab and Jewish names with positive or negative trait words, they were more likely to show positive attitudes toward Jewish people (by pressing keys with positive trait words) when tested in Hebrew than in Arabic.

Language promotes empathy: the quality that enables us to understand why people think and behave as they do. Bilingual children perform better on tests that require them to understand a situation from someone else's perspective—possibly because their brains are habituated to switching between two languages.

Language changes the physical structure of molecules in our bodies. A Japanese scientist found that words can change the physical structure of water; altering the shapes of the crystals that they form.

Language influences ageing. Yes, seriously. Language influences ageing so profoundly that experts now rank it alongside smoking, nutrition, exercise, and rest as a determinant of ageing. In the study, a group of elderly people were hosted at a one-week retreat where the décor, food, TV programs, and newspapers were the same as they would have been in the 1950s. The guests were instructed to act and talk as if they were really living in that decade. A second group also spent the week in the time capsule, but were not instructed to talk in a way that suited the time period. After a week, both groups reported improvements in mood, but the group who "talked younger" showed lower blood pressure, better eyesight and hearing, and sharper cognitive abilities than before the experiment. Many had improved flexibility, and some had even gained height through improved posture.

Language is the original social technology and driving force of evolution. It is what makes us human. Yes, indeed: "In the beginning was the Word." Our species *homo sapiens* came into existence when our Neanderthal ancestors developed the gene which enabled language, FOXP2. None of our Neanderthal cousins (all six lineages of them) had language. Unable to avoid conflict or work together, share knowledge, build on the achievements of predecessors, make deals or benefit from the complementary resources of their neighbors, they became extinct. Language is the reason we survived, thrived, and went on to create cathedrals and computers, crisps and coffee cups, while worms—with whom we share 70 percent of our DNA—are still wriggling about in the earth, just as they were thousands of years ago. Just as they will be in another thousand years, while our successors are taking day trips to Mars, chewing freeze-dried ice cream, and goggling out the window.

So it wasn't so crazy, after all, to wonder whether my exposure to many languages might be the reason I couldn't join the fit of fire and fury over wait times at Heathrow airport. Language—the stuff of thought—does indeed influence our perception. And my thoughts were shaped by many and different languages to most people in that queue. Language created you and me, shapes our thinking and interactions, and enables our progress. Those moments in Heathrow, Nepal, and Sierra Leone were just small snapshots of the larger story of what it is to be human. Which is, it turns out, to be in possession of a kind of superpower that can change your life, and our world.

And all of it got me thinking: What if certain words (re) wire our brain for happiness? What if I could compile the words that helped me to notice beautiful things, accept the things I wouldn't choose, and stay sane in stressful situations? Might that be helpful to the growing numbers of people experiencing anxiety and depression?

What if they were foreign words, and sharing them had the happy side effect of generating understanding and appreciation of people from different countries and cultures, races, and religions? Might that help us to adapt to diversity? Could demonstrating the value of knowledge transmitted by minority languages help to assert the dignity of minority cultures; healing the harm caused by the destruction of languages? What if it helped to protect the world's 3,000 endangered languages, and the wisdom they contain— including knowledge about how to manage natural resources, resolve conflict, survive and thrive in particular environmental, political, and social conditions. Could protecting and sharing that knowledge help us in this time of change and challenge?

Didn't someone say that "words are our most inexhaustible source of magic, capable of both inflicting injury and remedying it?" Didn't someone else say that "language is the light of the mind," capable of illuminating the path to a better world? And didn't someone say that we must "carefully watch our words, because they become our actions," and our destiny? Yes . . . yes they did: Mahatma Gandhi, John Stuart Mill, and Albus Dumbledore. *Hmmm . . . Hmm . . .*

Well then . . . what if . . . what if I could create a platform to share foreign words that promote happiness, ease with diversity, and effective action to address challenges like climate change?

Terrible idea. Rubbish. Nope. Sounds mad. Don't do that. Definitely, do not do that. Whatever you do, do not do that. You've already got a job, and you haven't got time, and you're not cut out for it—but don't worry about that, because it's a terrible idea.

Over cocktails at a casino at Lake Tahoe, I decided to do it anyway. But for one reason only. Only for you. Only for you to be happy. Happier, at any rate. Because that's all a better world is, anyway—you and me and billions of others being happy. Till all the seas run dry, there will be days like these. Days when the café runs out of flaxseed muffins, and the news is all wildfires, and Boko Haram attacks, and melting ice caps and rising sea levels threatening to sweep away island nations, and some sort of crisis—political or environmental or economic or social or a war announced on snapchat—and you step away from your desk to grab a sandwich and return to find that all hell has broken loose. And there's no escape. Nowhere to go. You are there with your feet in your shoes, surveying the scene with the brain in your head and the pleasures, possibilities, and potential that it sees—or doesn't.

And how all of this goes is up to you.

William Shakespeare said, "These dark times will turn us all to fools and madmen." Except it's not true, is it? We have a choice. Dark times have always been there—always, right before the dawn—and in them, always, there are people who stay sane and shine bright, being the lighthouses who help us to find our way.

I offer the words in this book so that you can be one of them. I hope that they will do for you what they have done for me: been pure sunshine illuminating the beauty of our planet and its people. I hope that these words give you access to some of their resilience and ability to enjoy the many reasons we *always* have to feel glad. As you use these words, you will notice them. And as if by magic—word magic—you will create, as you speak, that better life that is the making of a better world. *Abracadabra!*

———

"Speak a new language, that the world may be a new world."
—Rumi

3

Tinogona

Tinogona (adj)

Pronunciation: tịnɒgɒnæ (tee-noh-goh-nah).

Origin: Shona (Zimbabwe), oral tradition.

Definition: "It is achievable." Connotes belief that all things are possible, even realizing apparently unreasonable, unattainable, and unrealistically ambitious objectives.

How to use *tinogona*

Use *tinogona* to put the pep in your step that comes from knowing that all things are possible. Life is full of miracles: happily improbable victories over limitation and misfortune and injustice—like catching a train when literally every traffic light was red in the taxi to the station, and the ticket machine was broken, and your watch fell off on the platform. *Tinogona.* Losing ten pounds even though you've got the hunger of a herd of wildebeest and intense cravings for Oreos and literally anything cookies-and-cream related. *Tinogona.* Holding a little gizmo made of plastic and metal and glass that gives instant access to all the world's knowledge as just one of its applications. *Tinogona.*

Human progress is a story of the realization of the crazy ideas of people who believed that they could, and you can be one of them. You can achieve your desires, despite the mind's doubts and the vigorous eye-rolling of people who can't imagine your vision. It's not for them to have your vision—they've got their own. They've got their plans and incentives; you've got yours. Let it be. Use *tinogona* to become a bit deaf to doubts and doubters (including the ones in your own mind).

Use *tinogona* to reassure yourself that you can. You can have that fancy pen or pair of yoga pants or beach house or Balmain jacket, if that's what you want. Through payment plans or careful saving or patient waiting for the sale, an unexpected gift or inheritance, *tinogona*. You can be a singer-songwriter or CEO or civil servant or engineer or entrepreneur or artist or architect or caregiver or community leader or roofer or writer or winner of Nathan's Hot Dog Eating Contest. Why not? J.K. Rowling is no "starving artist." Ai Weiwei isn't toiling in obscurity. Beyoncé's bank balance is fine. Someone's winning Grammys and scholarships and promotions and proposals and prizes and contracts and the heart of a gorgeous person, and it might as well be you. I know, I know. Maybe you don't know how to make it happen (yet). Me neither. Even so, *tinogona*. We will find a way, or we will make one. Heck, you might get your lucky break standing in line at Starbucks.

Use *tinogona* to feel the hope that comes from knowing that miracles like that are part of nature. They happen all the time—especially for those with the hope and chutzpah, confidence and creativity, patience and persistence, sustained by the belief contained in this one word: *tinogona.* Use it to win.

How I discovered *tinogona*

These pages are the first thing I have ever written with a Tiffany pen. A solid sterling silver Tiffany pen, no less. A silver pen that I withdrew from a soft velvet Tiffany blue pouch on which Tiffany & Co. is printed—in gold lettering, naturally.

A Tiffany pen that belongs to me. Yep, little ole me who doesn't even have a job contract at the moment. Me who knows better than to covet such a thing—rod of rabid materialism! Quill of conspicuous consumption!—but who has seen the adverts of Carolyn Murphy resplendent and sparkling, and is not immune to their power. And so between you and me, I'm delighted with my shiny superfluity.

When I'm enlightened, I won't mind a bit about such things. I'll float about in an old sack with as much pleasure as a de la Renta gown, carrying a clump of charcoal with no less pleasure. Until then, I'm all "Check me out, I finally got this thing I've wanted for years!" Hopping around on one leg in a circle, clicking my fingers with one hand and pumping the pen in the air with the other.

It cost fifty dollars in a thrift shop.

A short trip up the Hudson River on a sleepy, sunny Sunday, and I wandered past a shop with crates and curios stacked on the sidewalk. I entered to buy a wooden box, squeezing between stacks of dusty books, bottles and tins, beads and toys, a skeleton and a suit of armor to the glass case counter at the back of the shop.

And there it was, lying like a lady on a chaise longue; atop the Tiffany blue pouch, atop an opened Tiffany blue box. That's how someone who was unemployed (in that moment) got the pen she had wanted for years.

Oh, I just saw it has "Tiffany & Co. Sterling 925" embossed on the shaft. I'm not sure what that means but couldn't be happier than if Audrey Hepburn came back from the dead and served me a croissant.

There is a word for such improbable happenings: *tinogona*. A Shona (Zimbabwe) word meaning "it is achievable," *tinogona* connotes the reality that even your most unreasonable objectives and impossible desires are "I'm possible." They are, in fact, daily occurrences. Delivering the assignment on time even though you needed another week and pair of hands, but had neither as the deadline approached; just the flu and a friend visiting, expecting to be entertained: *tinogona*. Driving thirty-four miles on an empty tank to the nearest petrol station: *tinogona*. Finding the keys to your apartment (so small!) in Central Park (so big!) with little more than a vague recollection that you might have left them near a tree that was an unusual color: *tinogona*. These are my recent triumphs; how about you?

Also—how many people can you fit in an old Toyata Hiace minibus?

Fifteen?

Well done! Here, have a biscuit. According to the manufacturer and common sense, you are right on the money.

Also: forty-five people, three babies, six goats, four chickens, nine sacks of coconuts, six suitcases, two backpacks, a sound system, and nine twelve-bottle crates of Chibuku Shake-Shake beer.

And that's how I learned about *tinogona*: on a battered bus bouncing through the savannahs and forests of Southeast Africa. I also learned that a very bruised bum becomes numb and can sit quite comfortably, actually, squidged next to another on a single seat. But that's not the point of this story. Let me tell you what is.

First of all, when I say "seat," I mean a scratched and holey piece of plastic stretched over a lattice of iron bars that once held a cushion. Alas, the cushion has lost its puff from the pounding of posteriors bouncing on bumpy roads ravaged by bombs. An unfortunate collision of circumstances: my bottom has also lost its puff after weeks without much food. On a good day, I can find a banana and a cup of tea in Zimbabwe. But most days, I must travel to a neighboring country (Botswana, Malawi) for pizza and a piece of cake. Not enough of either, clearly: baggy jeans strapped to me with a spare cord from my backpack as my bony buttocks crash into potholes, and bounce over holes filled but not smoothed over.

I reflect on the numb-bum blessing as I sit, two to a seat, holding my neighbor's baby on my lap. There are bags and cases under our feet, and zero possibility of moving our legs for several hours. Still, we are better off than the goat under the seat, and the chicken in a loosely tied black plastic bag by my left foot, which bleat and flap as we go. Better off too than the guy with my knees jammed into his crotch as he crouches by the door, surveying we passengers for spare inches between, below, behind, in front of us—anywhere that an extra person, animal, or piece of luggage can be squeezed. Space is money, and it's his job to fill it: packing people in, even when you think there is not one square inch left.

And surely now, there is not one square inch left.

Take me for example: I have a few crates of mini beer bottles jammed into my ribs. On top of these: a suitcase. On top of this: a few sheets of plastic with sharp corners that are jabbing into my neck. And on top of these: my backpack. At our last stop, a case wedged behind the backpack pushed it into my face, forcing my head to the side and straight into the sack of coconuts now pressed into my nose and forehead. And would you believe it? This is prime minibus real estate: the Mayfair of the minibus. The young man sitting next to me has his face in the armpit of a gentleman whose head and neck are curved around and pressed against the roof.

We have traveled like this—face in armpit, knee in crotch, bottles in ribs, plastic in neck, face in sack, skull to ceiling—for about five hours, and I am convinced: this is it. There is no more room.

The bus slows. Worried, I ask my neighbor for information. Apparently, a couple standing on the side of the red earth road has hailed the bus. They have a baby and a basin of dried fish and some luggage. Ah, right. Obviously, the driver is stopping out of politeness, to say, "Nah. Sorry folks, not going to happen. There's no space here for another thing."

But what do I know? I do not yet have faith to move mountains. I have not yet learned that all things—even fitting forty-something folk and their livestock and luggage in a fifteen-seater—are *tinogona*. Not yet. I need five more minutes. Five minutes for this to happen: the minibus stops. The guy with my knee in his crotch maneuvers carefully to untangle our limbs, opens the door, and greets the couple. He takes their two smaller bags, raises the windscreen wipers, and passes the bag handles over the blades. He climbs onto the roof and rearranges the people and goats up there to make room for more passengers. He opens the back of the bus and crams in their cases. Since this space is not designed to store anything at all, it will not now close. No problem!

He passes ropes up and around the entire vehicle to keep the contents inside. *Tinogona.* Since it's quite hot on this summer's day in sub-Saharan Africa, and a basin of dried fish is a suboptimal travel companion, our hero opens the door and places his arms and legs over it—like a starfish—so all the humans and goats and chickens and coconuts and cases stay in. Air conditioning? *Tinogona.*

And we're off! Back door open, ropes tied, bags swaying from windscreen-wipers, passengers crammed, chickens flapping, goats bleating, music cranked up, and *tinogona*: forty-five people, three babies, six goats, four chickens, nine sacks of coconuts, six suitcases, two backpacks, a sound system, and nine twelve-bottle crates of Chibuku Shake-Shake in a fifteen-seater minibus.

We travel over 300 kilometers this way, in a country with a fuel crisis. *Tinogona.* We are now in Masvingo, home of the Great Zimbabwe ruins: ancient stone walls, towers, and fortresses built by Shona cattlemen over seven centuries ago, and still standing. Still standing after seven centuries of wind and rain, even though no mortar was used in construction and the rocks are bound by nothing at all. *Tinogona.*

They have stood through the realization of many more impossible dreams. Freedom for colonized peoples. Rights for women, persons with disabilities, and people of color. The end of the Atlantic slave trade, eradication of smallpox, invention of the printing press, the combustion engine, the motorcar, the lightbulb, the airplane, the internet, the iPhone. At one time, all of these seemed impossible. Why would members of Parliament, representing cities whose wealth came from the slave trade, vote to end it? Why would male, wealthy, and educated people dilute their power by granting votes to others? Why would firms whose whole business model is based on exploiting fossil fuels go all-in on green energy?

"Naïve nonsense!"

"Dangerous delusions!"

"Have you ever heard anything so ridiculous in all your born days?"

"No I have not! Not since that Copernicus chap insisted that the sun was the center of the universe!"

And yet . . .

And yet we live in a world in which all of this happened—doubts and doubters be damned. So next time you think the world is going to hell in a handbasket, and we can't possibly address the challenges we face, remember that. Remember it when you think of doing that thing that appears to sparkle in your mind; exciting then scaring you as you reel off (or hear) all the reasons why you shouldn't and can't and it's not realistic or financially viable. Imagine what the Wright brothers' neighbors thought of their efforts to fly about in a steel box.

"Bloody lunatics."

"Yes exactly. Totally mad."

"Dangerous, I say."

"Very! Their poor mother must be worried sick. Some more tea, dear?"

And yet . . .

And yet, here you are, wondering when to take that trip to Bali.

Funny, that.

"And for goodness' sake, that Beethoven! He's deaf, for crying out loud! Why doesn't he just try to paint or something?!"

And yet . . .

And yet, here we are in our world made better by the achievement of impossible dreams. A world to be made even better by the achievement of yours. *Tinogona.*

———

"First they ignore you. Then they ridicule you . . . then they build monuments to you. And that is what is going to happen."
—Nicholas Klein

4

Tu'u-lun

> **Tu'u-lun** (noun)
>
> **Pronunciation**: 'tü 'lün (too-oo-loon).
>
> **Origin**: Tetun (Timor Lorosa'e, also known as Timor Leste or East Timor, Asia Pacific).
>
> **Definition**: Help; support; collaboration; joint effort; shared achievement.

How to use *tu'u-lun*

"Oh . . . but I don't want to be a burden . . ."

"You're so busy, I don't want to bother you."

"It's okay, I guess I'll just . . . do it on my own."

"Don't worry, I can do it myself."

No, you can't.

You are talented and brilliant, and in every way excellent—no doubt about it. Not from me, anyway. You're reading my book, and I wholeheartedly approve of everything about you. Except this: the strong independent (wo)man thing.

"If you want something done well, do it yourself."

"When you laugh, the whole world laughs with you, when you cry, you cry alone."

In these few words is a recipe for failure in all its forms. And you deserve better than that—because, like I say, you have all these good qualities and possibilities and are generally excellent, just as you are. It's just that your potential is limited by your support, and if you only asked for it, you'd be better off. Nothing personal, my dear, it's just the way it is: alone we are strong; together we are stronger.

Whatever you want to do, I can promise you two things. One: you can do it. Two: you can't do it alone. Your challenge—in addition to fine-tuning your talents on the trombone or trapeze or trading or whatever—is to find the complementary skills, talents, networks you need to realize your vision. Marketing experts, mentors, advisers, social media whizzes . . . we all need many kinds of support to get to where we want to be. Power exists in people, and the connections between them. So most likely, you're going to have to make some more of them.

I know, I know. You'd rather poke your eyes out than ask for help. But remember: we all benefit from collaboration. People like to make a bit of money, contribute to the well-being of another person, or simply be part of the "something beautiful" that is the realization of your vision. Whose idea of a good time is to sit around doing nothing, alone, forever? Exactly.

Tu'u-lun is a Timorese word meaning "help, support, collaboration, joint endeavor, shared achievement." Use it to gee up yourself to ask for help, knowing that any big success is a collaborative endeavor; asking for support is a sign of strength (not of weakness); and that when you do, you might just be doing the person you ask a favor as well. Heck, you might even make a friend for life. And if that turns out not to be the case? Well then, they can say "no," and you can move on.

So are we over the "I've got to do it all by myself" thing yet? Yes? No?

Here's a recap: You need support. You need to ask for it.

And asking for it isn't a bummer—it's a boon. Because when the work is done, the project launched, the product released, the ribbon cut, the "grab and grin" shot, the last box unloaded, the chairs stacked, the "and that's a wrap (*woo!*)" announced—the party begins.

And a party? Well now . . . a little party never hurt anybody. Pop!

How I discovered *tu'u-lun*

It's tea time on Islay, a small island off the West Coast of Scotland, and we're having a chat.

"So how're you gettin' on in America?" asks Mary from Number 6, handing me tea and a treat: a Tunnock's Teacake resting against the side of the tea cup.

Mmm . . . it'll be nice and melty inside.

Between sips of sweet, milky tea and bites of molten marshmallow, I tell her about all things America. From scones: "Sweet?!! Are they really?! supposed to be more of a bread really, isn't it, a scone?"—to subway dancers: "Clonk you on the head?! Deary me! That's not what you want, is it?!"—and doctors considered almost like Gods: "Is that right? Funny isn't it. We need doctors, no doubt about it. But where'd we be without the shopkeepers and the lighthouse keepers and the dustmen and the delivery drivers and the folk who run the ferry and the fishermen and the farmers and the folk who work in the pub and the post office and the bank and *och!* Where'd we be without everybody, really?"

And who can say it isn't true? An island of doctors or lawyers or any single profession just would not work.

Then we got talking about biscuits the size of your head: "Oh aye! they call them cookies, don't they?" Burgers so big that they need to be held together with a cocktail stick: "How do you actually eat that then?" And that was that. I didn't think about it again until I went to another island years later: Timor Leste.

T-what?

Timor Leste. East Timor. *Timor Lorosae* ("Land of the Rising Sun"). An island paradise between Indonesia and Australia, five to eleven days away from Scotland (by plane). Due to bizarre occurrences like a volcanic eruption and the plane crew pausing to go surfing and insects on the runway, poor, poor me was stranded en route in Bali for weeks at a time, eating pounds of jack fruit and getting so many massages that I developed varicose veins. That was the first surprise in a job that was full of them. For there are many surprising things about the National Police of Timor Leste.

In the middle of the Office of the Commander General is a twenty-five-foot live crocodile named Maria. Yes, according to Timorese folklore, a crocodile is good luck. Sort of like one of those waving cats in a Chinese restaurant, but much higher maintenance. Each ministry has one apparently. Maria's brother is at the Ministry of Defense, she has a cousin at the Ministry of Education, etc.

"Is that . . . ," I ask, rubbernecking my way up the stairs to meet the team, "is that . . . a crocodile?"

"Maria, you mean? You can feed her if you want."

At the top of the stairs is a UN project run by a war hero who works side-by-side with people who imprisoned and tortured him and killed a number of his family members. One day, I asked him about it. All he said was these few words with a shrug of the shoulders: "Of course, isn't it? We all need each other."

Strategic Planning Day brought low, mid, and high-ranking officers from all over the country, caterers and cleaners, folk from the clinic and garage together with the Commander General and Minister of Defense to jointly decide how to improve the police service. They discussed everything from fleet management to crocodile pool maintenance with a few breaks for sips and snacks: deep-fried bananas (midmorning), deep-fried fish (lunch), and in the afternoon, deep-fried samosas and a bread basket. My eyes shone upon the bread. Bread! A non-deep-fried item!

Alas, no. Doughnut batter, filled with mince and deep fried. I chewed slowly, in a daze, eyes goggling because I've never seen anything like it. Not just the deep-fried peanuts: the collaboration. Usually, in a country affected by some sort of crisis, recovery is led by a relatively small number of senior officials who live and work in gated and guarded compounds. They travel between them in Toyota Land Cruisers and tend, inevitably, to use their own ideas, education, and experiences to design policies, programs, and plans to promote peace and progress for "all the people" of (insert name of country here). When they tried that in Timor, it didn't go so well. And when I say it didn't go so well, I mean, the people burned the place down. Yes, the Timorese are so convinced that "we all need each other" that they torched their own capital—even after twenty-four years of fighting to free it from Indonesian occupation. It was a war won through collaboration among the country's many ethnic groups, international supporters, highly revered ancestors, and spirits of the land. And they burned it down in protest against an international administration that failed to respect the importance of this principle.

"Where'd we be without everybody?" Gasping and squinting as tires burn and sirens scream.

From these two islands on either side of our blue-and-green earth, I learned *tu'u-lun*. It's a word from Tetun (the main language of Timor L'orosa'e) meaning help, support, collaborative endeavor, joint effort, shared achievement, *tu'u-lun* connotes the reality that to achieve big success of any kind, we need to unite. Only by drawing in complementary skills, resources, and capacities can we create the combined force that makes us equal to the challenges we face.

Quite why I needed to learn it, I don't know. It's obvious really. You aren't growing the bananas in your fruit bowl or fishing the cod in your fridge, or installing the grid that brings electricity to your home. You probably don't often think about the Oscars' speech length list of people that make life good. On an island, you can't *not* think about it. There's Angus the farmer, and Clive in the post office, and Katherine in the bank, and Campbell the fencer, and Peter in the pub, and Tosh the dustman, and Andrew the electrician, and Mary—who was a nurse but now runs the quilting club—and James who runs the Pipe Band, and Gordon in the mill, and John in the shop, and Nick the plumber, and Sam the painter, and Maggie the teacher, and Arthur who runs the wee boat to Jura, and so on. And you probably saw a good few of them in a single morning, popping into the shop for the papers and a pint of milk.

At some point, one of them may use the phrase: "Aye right!" a sarcastic Scot's response to someone you suspect may be telling you a *loadae nonsense*. Islanders know, you see. They know that there's a crucial distinction between what's true, and what we're told—and that quite a lot of what we're told is a *loadae nonsense*. Take Darwin, for example. How many have labored under the illusion that competition drives progress? How many have placed two fearfully protective arms around their projects and struggled on solo on the grounds that "If you want something done well, do it yourself?"

How many have thought female/foreign/Jewish/Black people were not wise or worthy enough to be included in their endeavors—even though the evidence shows that diverse teams out-perform, out-innovate and out-earn all others?

How many have construed asking for help as an expression of weakness or nuisance and never done the hugely important, impactful thing that they could have done?

How many have considered soliciting support as inappropriate to their gender, or place in a hierarchy, and slogged before sunrise and after sunset, through Saturday and Sunday, into a sadly solitary celebration-free existence sustained by vending machine meals in front of a screen?

"Loadae nonsense!"

Yes, islanders have long known what evolutionary biologists only just discovered: Darwin was wrong. Turns out that collaboration, not competition, is the driving force of human evolution, and our current rate of progress is, as ever, a function of our level of collaboration. From cutting peat and pulling a cow out of a bog, to freeing a nation and figuring out what the heck is happening with fleet management, you're going to need reinforcement. The image of the fearless leader single-handedly changing the world—Martin Luther King, Mahatma Gandhi, Simon Bolivar, and what not—is a *loadae nonsense!* Behind each of them was a movement of many millions of people, and "their" successes belonged to each and every one of those millions.

Ours is a time to unite across the boundaries of country, culture, race, and religion, to harness a collective strength that is equal to the challenges we all face: climate change and conflict, poverty and inequality, discrimination and (let's face it) the after effects of being at home for a year and a half, with little more exciting to do than watch Netflix and go for a walk around the block with all the other new dog owners. It is a time for big new ideas to address them. Bold ideas from new people and places. Your ideas—IF you realize them. And you realize them through *tu'u-lun.*

Here's the problem: a good number of us would rather eat a pound of deep-fried peanuts than risk creating a partnership. Obviously, some are just a piece of work, and are welcome to chew through a few pounds of indigestible snacks. For the rest of us: GOOD NEWS! Almost everything you think about asking for help—that maybe, if you only work hard enough, you can avoid it; that it makes you a pest; that you mustn't burden people (they're busy enough); that your place is to help others and make their lives easier, and their success possible (not the other way around)—is a *loadae nonsense*.

When you ask for help (and if you're doing anything remotely interesting or impactful, then you're going to have to), you actually give the person you are asking an opportunity to be more successful, healthy, and happy. Leaving aside the pay or profit or prestige that collaborating with you can bring, research shows that whether or not a person volunteers is a more accurate indicator of mental and physical well-being than level of income, exercise, cholesterol, and blood pressure. Research also shows that money given away brings more pleasure than money spent on ourselves, and that even simply listening to another person (listening even to their troubles) leads to the firing of neurons and a flow of oxytocin (the "love hormone") that brings the same happy glow as you get from a lovely hug, a warm bath, or cozy chat on a softened sofa with Mary, sipping tea and munching the molten marshmallow of a mighty Tunnock's Teacake.

And you know what else? Studies from places that experience war and environmental disaster consistently show that our ability to survive and recover from shocks is a function of social connectedness: the strengthen of our links to neighbors, family, friends, and the institutions to serve us all. Our mental, emotional, and physical resilience depends on them; and our joy is fed by them.

When you put it all together, it starts to look like the poets and the priests were right: you and I were born to love.

Born with many needs, to be met by many people. Born to seek your own happiness, and to find it in contributing to the happiness of others. Born to give to others, and to receive from others in a flow of support that sustains success in all its forms. Born imperfect and incomplete, dependent and destined to create the person-to-person connections that are the perfection of life.

So here's to you, my dear: to your imperfection, to the connections they motivate, and to the *tu'u-lun* that will underpin your success. Pop!

———

"Our success increasingly depends on the strength of our relationships with each other." —Hugh Verrier

5

Poze

How to use *poze*

Rise and grind! Slay the day! Hustle like a boss! Adrenalin coursing through your veins, caffeine stimulating every nerve, EDM pumping through your earphones, and you're ready to attack the twenty-first century equivalent of a lion: your to-do list. *ARGHHHHHHHHH!! RAARR!!!* WATCH OUT, WORLD! I'M COMING!!!!!!!!! I know you are. Of course you are. I know it. She knows it. He knows it. Your mum definitely knows it. We all know it. We see your shine and sparkle and how much you have to offer the world. Own it, flaunt it, work it; but for goodness' sake, please don't kill yourself over it. Just note down all the small things you must do to achieve your big objective, and then do them, one after the other, with confidence in others and faith in yourself. It's a marathon, not a sprint, so you can afford to chill out a bit.

I know, it doesn't come easy to me either, but please know that practically everyone else has discovered this truth, and we're falling behind like the hare in Aesop's fable because we're not paying attention to it. Are you ready? Good, here it is: Peace is a productive state.

You can use the Haitian Creole word *poze* to access it. Meaning relaxed, peaceful, at ease, Haitians say "*poze*" in response to "*kouman ou ye?*" ("How are you?"), to let you know they are feeling good. Or they'll say it to you when you look a bit frazzled, stressed, or simply moving too fast to be able to reach your goal. A combination of relax, chill out, and take it easy, *poze* is Caribbean linguistic medicine for anxiety. Use it to take the time to notice the pleasures around you, become relaxed enough to think clearly about your next steps, and set yourself up for a positive and productive day.

Tolstoy wrote that "[t]he two most powerful warriors are patience and time." It turns out that actual warriors, the ones who find themselves facing a barrage of gunfire, agree with the Haitians: we are more successful when we chill out a bit. As the British military expression goes: "There's always time for a Hamlet." A Hamlet, in case you're wondering, is a small cigar. It takes a few minutes to smoke—sufficient time to become calm enough to find a way through a crisis. But by all means, make yourself a matcha or an origami crane or something. Whatever it takes for you to get relaxed: to become the version of yourself that is able to achieve all those things on your to-do list (and the bigger dream that they add up to).

There's a scientific underpinning for what the Haitians learned from over two hundred years of overcoming troubles not limited to slavery, earthquakes, typhoons, tornados, tropical storms, torrential rains, cyclones, floods, armed conflict, violent coups, economic collapse, dictatorships, disease, poverty, hyperinflation, and hurricanes. Studies show that when we are relaxed, our brain produces slower waves which heighten concentration, imagination, memory, learning, and creativity. The mind can more easily find simple solutions to stressful situations, focus and stay on task. Our butts can stay in the chair long enough to finish. Faster brain waves make you active and alert, able to rapidly process information, reason, and outrun a tiger. But get too caught up in the hustle-and-guzzle caffeine M.O. that we often equate with being productive, and an excess of these faster waves zaps our focus, making us stressed, anxious and restless, while obliterating our energy, emotional awareness, creativity, and life span. Bummer.

You may well get sh*t done, but also look, feel, and act a bit sh*t yourself after you slump on the sofa, nerves frayed, and struggling to hold in an outburst about dinner or the dishwasher or why is it always me that has to do everything???!!!!! There is an alternative to this sorry scenario: breathe.

Breathe deeply. Deep breath in and deep breath out, to enter the relaxed alpha brain wave state and activate the parasympathetic nervous system, so your body can recover from that incident with the tiger and the dishwasher tablets. There you go, feeling better? This is *poze*, my friend. It's how to feel your best (calm, peaceful), be your best (kind, appreciative) self, do your best (creative, inspired) work, and notice the best of this precious day that will never come again. Not lazy, not remiss, not in need a shot of caffeine and a kick in the pants: just *poze*. Peaceful. Positive. Productive. Pretty much perfect.

How I discovered *poze*

Saturday in the park. By 9:30 a.m., a hundred or so half-marathoners were gearing up for personal bests: stretching and slurping down caffeine-carb packs, slathering on sunscreen, readjusting sports watches, fiddling with compression socks. One guy was gyrating in a sweat band; a few others were stretching or shrugging and waving and rotating their arms about in every direction, looking like they're playing "Eye of the Tiger" in their head. They had what Swedes call *resfeber*: that mixture of anxiety and excitement before an important journey. Arms stretched, heads cocked from side to side, laces tightened.

9:45. Almost time. At 9:53, Matthew arrived in a pair of swim shorts and a Willie Nelson T-shirt, cup of Maker's Mark in hand. He moved slowly, smoking. He grinned broadly at a few acquaintances, high fived the pacers, smoked that cigarette right down to the tip, knocked back the rest of his bourbon, and finished the course in ninety minutes.

He is what Haitians call *poze*: relaxed and calm, still and peaceful, poised and productive. He is probably also what English speakers call "high," but well, that's not an important part of this story.

The important part of this story takes place in Miami airport, as full-of-beans, reach-for-the-moon, development workers board the plane for the Haitian capital Port-au-Prince, to begin their mission to end poverty/environmental degradation/child abuse or some other offence to human dignity. On the island itself, I could see who those new arrivals would apparently become: exhausted, fed-up, tired, irritated by any inconvenience (which was almost everything) and *DONE.* And then there were the Haitians: peacefully untroubled by life. Hanging out. Doing what they needed to do—including implementing those donor-funded projects to end poverty/environmental degradation/child abuse and so on—but with much less gurning, grimacing, teeth clenching, and brow-furrowing than their international counterparts. My friend Adrienne called it. After two years in Port Salut, a coastal town in the South coast of the country, she had seen the same scene long enough to notice its details and learn its lesson. Sitting in a Sunday sun dress with toes in the sand and a beer in hand as a warm Caribbean Sea breeze blew over the bay, she said, "You know, we're here trying to improve all these countries, but I think they really have it figured out in a lot of ways. There's something in this *poze* thing."

Poze. You'll hear it all the time in Haiti. *"Kouman ou ye?"* ("How are you?") If someone responds to this question, as they often will, with *"poze,"* you know he or she is feeling fit and fine. Optimal. Even if their goat is chewing on a plastic bottle, and you have questions about what the heck their family are eating today, Haitians trust that being *poze* is the way to figure out the answer to that and other questions. And if you should in any way start to headless chicken it about the place, trying to force reality to conform to your expectations so you can MAKE SURE that food and water and electricity and fuel and the chickens and goats and internet are where and when and how you want them to be, Haitians will remind you that the way to achieve that—even in this context where it seems that damn near everything is against you—is to chill out a bit.

"*Poze! poze!*" ("Relax! Take it easy!"). Yep. Slow down. Breathe, baby. Easy does it.

Haitians know a thing or two about how to do the impossible with the available. Around two hundred years ago, they fought and won a war against one of the strongest nations on earth—France—to free themselves from slavery. And every year since then, they've had to overcome some sort of disaster: earthquake, typhoon, tornado, cyclone, tropical storm, torrential rain, flood, war, coup, dictatorship, disease contested election, or economic collapse. And did I mention the hurricanes? Yes: eleven of them since 1998. With the majority of the population living on less than US$2.41 per day, Haitians, perhaps more than most of the people on our planet, have to bring an almost unimaginable level of creativity to the daily challenge of surviving and finding some things to smile about. It's a remarkable resourcefulness that passes from parent to child over generations, and it is encapsulated in this one four letter word: *poze.*

The received wisdom of millions of Haitians now has a scientific underpinning. Neuroscientists have found that when we are relaxed, our brains produce slower waves, which heighten concentration, imagination, memory, and learning. These alpha, theta, and delta waves enable us to focus and stay on task, and to make smart decisions under pressure. Curious about what it takes to perform well under pressure, psychologists collaborated with people who rely on that skill to stay alive: military commanders, emergency responders, police officers, polar explorers, and mountaineers.

What did they discover?

That when a military operation is going wrong, or there's an avalanche at high altitude, the key to finding smart solutions is to pause, step back, and reflect.

Yes. Even in those extreme situations, *poze* is the key to success.

Haitians know that the purpose of *poze* is to amplify your power, making you equal to the challenges you face. *Poze* makes us smart enough to find our way out, around or through them; and strong enough to endure them with a smile and a swagger. *Poze* empowers us to make the impossible, possible; to find a way or to make one with guts and grace. After all, there is always a way forward for the person with the courage to relax just enough to find it, under the lifting fog of fear and fury.

So Haitians don't worry one bit about being at ease. They don't respond to a peaceful, relaxed state with a guilty grimace and trip to the coffee machine as they wonder about low iron levels. Nope. Haitians feel no concern about being *poze* (except perhaps how to get there).

Because, along with yogis and martial artists, they know the secret that a relaxed state is a productive state. Productive and happy—though in our Starbucks-ified world, you may struggle to believe it. We've got:

- Psyched up and ready to attack the to-do list, and
- Relaxed and ready to do nothing more than turn the volume up on the TV.

And yet it is true: peace is a productive state.

Think of a baby. A beautiful little thing taking it easy: lying around for months, sleeping, eating, goggling at all the giant people cuddling, patting, and soaping him. Just chillin'. Chillaxin. Doubling in size every few months and rapidly acquiring the same core skills as a whole adult human. So very *poze*, and so very productive: rapidly becoming like the giant person soaping him in the sink.

Think of Einstein: sitting by the window on the tram in Bern. Just chillin. Chillaxin. Coming up with the theory of relativity.

Yes, peace is a productive state. Productive also because it enables you to directly feel the happiness that is the whole point of existence; the ultimate objective of everything you do and want. *Poze* is a way to feel those happy-for-no-reason good vibes that are available to us anyway, whether or not you win the race, or get the prize, or retrofit the house to withstand another earthquake or hurricane. It's a state that we can reach through achieving our goals, yes—but also just while swinging in a hammock or peeling carrots; spinning prayer wheels in a Tibetan monastery, or waiting at the bus stop in Slough. Very important: the happiness that is the ultimate end of human existence is accessible to all of us, everywhere. The Dalai Lama and Richard Gere and Madonna and Sting and the people of Haiti and you and me. All with the same opportunities to feel peace; the same challenge to feel *poze*.

Yes, the same. I know, I know: those guys get to practice peace in a poof of incense in a wellness ashram in Pondicherry, while you have to try in the driving rain at a train station on the outskirts of Aberdeen—how is that the same? Because you both want to scratch your skin off. Peace takes effort, especially for those of us hoodwinked into believing that if you don't feel stressed and awful, then you're not working hard enough. Sure, you can cheat your way to it like Matt and most of us, but it doesn't work. What goes up must come down. True peace can't be smoked or sniffed or sipped or popped or puffed or munched or molten on your tongue. It takes effort. Gentle effort, consistent effort, grounded in the knowledge that peace is a productive state.

What about if you've got a BIG GOAL? Dreams. Big dreams, baby. A purpose. A mission. A GREAT THING to do. An important contribution to the collective cultural, economic, social, wealth of society. Ending poverty or environmental degradation or child abuse or something. Making some fantastic masterpiece that sets the world aflame with delight. What about that? You haven't got the luxury of chilling out and swinging in a hammock or spinning prayer wheels or whatever. You're different. You've got work to do—hustling and slaying and grinding to be one of the greats.

Yes indeed. I see. You're not going just for small pleasures; you're going for the supreme happiness that comes from fulfilling your life's purpose. Well, we each have one, of course: a unique and equally important role to play in the making of an even better world. It may be brokering a peace agreement, it may be setting up a company, it may be making the ultimate sandwich; each one of us has a job to do—one that is enjoyable, compelling, and will contribute to *tikkun olam*: the spiritual and political reformation of the world (Hebrew).

Say what? The spiritual and political reformation of the world? *Umm* . . . not sure what that means and pretty sure it's not up to me. Me I just want to set up my T-shirt printing company . . .

Yes, it is. Making this world an even better place is up to you and me. But we can all chill out about it. For one thing, we can more easily figure out what our purpose is when *poze*. A relaxed mind is a creative mind; the one that has all the great ideas in the shower.

For another, that lofty goal, a contribution to the betterment of mankind, is really no biggie. All great achievements chunk down to small accomplishments anyway: fill the form, prepare the budget, draft the web copy, draw up the itinerary, write the pitch, practice the performance. All these small accomplishments are more easily achieved when *poze*. A tranquil person can sit still long enough and focus well enough to do the many tasks on the to-do list of the big idea. None of these tasks are beyond any of us; it's just much harder to shovel through them when we are what Germans call *fisselig* (flustered to the point of incompetence) by the length of said to-do list, mentally looping the reasons we can't do them and ways we might be able to do them but OMG it's just too, too much, and there isn't enough time, and there just aren't enough people and . . .

And all this mental marathoning while physically running between meetings and the coffee machine and the water cooler as if we've got ants in our pants, complaining about this person and that unit and the flippin' printer, my goodness if we can't get the basics right how can we manage 6 percent growth this quarter, *hmmm*?! And over there in the corner, Paul is sitting at his desk, getting the hell on with it. And we don't like *poze* Paul because—well, he seems nice enough, but a bit odd.

And he is. A *poze* person is odd in a culture that equates success with stress, attainment with caffeination, and accomplishment with aggression. But nonetheless, it is true: peace is a productive state. Productive because it enables you to enjoy the lovely things around you all the time, and which add delight to your days—if you notice them.

What do you mean, lovely things around me all the time? Nope. Not right now: I've barely slept and I've got to be up and out and on parade again in a few hours. #riseandgrind #slaytheday #hustlelikeaboss. Frankly I feel awful. Definitely not got time for gazing at flower petals or reading Wordsworth (bleary eye roll).

I get you. By all means #slay and #hustle and go for the big dream, but right now . . . see that? There is *şafak* (Turkish): the soft glow of first light. *Raxeira* (Galician): sun rays that form as light filters through the window on a rainy day. *Støvfnug* (Danish): dust flakes dancing in those rays. *Gökotta* (Swedish): morning birdsong. *Aamukaste* (Finnish): dew sparkling like jewels on branches and blades of grass. *Komorebi* (Japanese): sunlight filtering through the leaves of trees. *Tzafrir* (Hebrew): gently refreshing morning breeze. The feeling of the shower on your skin; your first sip of tea; the driver giving way; the person holding the door open; flowers at reception. So many reasons to feel good right now—if you are *poze* enough to notice. And now that you feel better—*TA DA!* You can do your best. (You're welcome).

So by all means, my *cosmopolitan* companion, pursue your purpose. Make a dent in the universe. Follow your passion. Play your part in the making of a better world. But take it lightly. Do it *poze*—calmly active, actively calm, then put down the tools and kick back with a book or a beer with buddies. Please don't reach for a Nespresso or a Haribo and try to squeeze another few hours' work out of yourself. *Poronkusema* is the Finnish word for the distance a reindeer can comfortably travel before needing a break. Well, you and every other living thing needs a break. Either you take that break, or you will break. Burnout: it's not pretty and neither is approaching the day as though it's some sort of battle between you and the to-do list. Forget those #slaytheday memes. What does that even mean? Today is not for slaying, it's for enjoying: enjoying work, enjoying rest, enjoying play—and *poze* helps you succeed at all of them. Sure, there are times when enjoyment seems a tall order, but even on days like these, no lion is going to chase you through the office. You don't need that level of adrenaline. You need peace. You need calm. You need to know you got this. And you do.

———

"Wisely and slow; they stumble that run fast." —William Shakespeare

6

Gozar

Gozar (verb)

Pronunciation: go'zar (goh-sahr).

Origin: Spanish (Spain, Latin America).

Definition: To enjoy; Latin *gaudeo* (I rejoice); to take pleasure; to have a ball; to feel good; to be carefree (possibly entering a state of flow where you lose track of time). Related: *Gozar + de*: to enjoy, to get a kick out of. *Gozar + con*: to take delight in. *Gozarse + en* hacer: to enjoy doing.

How to use *gozar*

BE HAPPY!!!!!! (smiley face). BE POSITIVE!!!!! (thumbs up).

A slightly dictatorial command to enter into a specific state, with the vague sense that there is something wrong with you until you do. Me, I don't know how to "BE HAPPY!!!!!!" or "BE POSITIVE!!!!!!" any more than I know how to "GET WELL AT ONCE!" while tossing feverishly in bed, surrounded by tissues and half-drunk cups of Lemsip: a much-loved British flu remedy.

Nothing wrong with BEing HAPPY!!!!!! and BEing POSITIVE!!!!! of course, and the positivity police are probably trying to be helpful. It's just that these trails of rainbow emojis, smileys, and bumper sticker messages are not specific enough to be helpful. What can we actually do in practice to enter this amorphous state?

Enter *gozar*: a Spanish word for the good feeling that comes from engaging in simple things that make you feel good. That's it. That's all. You just do something, with your mind or body, that gives you pleasure. When you are feeling low, do something to uplift yourself. It could be chatting to someone or putting on a good tune. It could be recalling a happy memory or anticipating a good moment to come. Watching a funny video or have a bath. Seeing the sunrise, the sunset, or sunlight on a leaf. Having a cup of your expensive tea, seeing flowers, smelling essential oils, reading a poem, kicking back with a beer, serving yourself a slice of cake, or closing the curtains, putting on a tune, and dancing like a maniac. It really just depends on what the moment requires. Sometimes it's a whiskey, sometimes a walk, sometimes it's declaring Wednesday over and watching TV in your underwear.

And when familiar thoughts arise: I haven't got time, I'm too tired, I haven't got anyone to do that with, they'll think I'm an idiot—ignore them. Ignore them all and do it anyway. Ignore them and do any simple, quick, easy, free, or cheap thing you can to make you feel good. This is *gozar*: doing simple, practical things that make you feel good, and help you do good too. *Sí!*

Evidence from hundreds of studies involving hundreds of thousands of people demonstrates that people who feel good, do better—in every aspect of life. Their marriages, friendships, community involvement, altruism, health, life expectancy, immunity, intelligence, income, productivity, accuracy, efficiency, exam results, sales, performance evaluations, job security, job satisfaction, motivation, energy, learning, cognition, creativity, and even eyesight are all superior. And *gozar* is sufficient to generate these benefits. You don't need a Grammy award, a golden Porsche, or a direct line to the CEO. You just need to do simple things that make you feel good.

It seems so unlikely, doesn't it? Unlikely, at any rate, for anyone trained in ye olde Western thinking that only if you work hard, achieve all your goals, get your qualifications, recognition, pension, etc., will you be happy—and possibly after retirement. Unlikely too for ye olde Eastern thinking that you'll be happy only if you devote enough effort to your spiritual practice—and possibly in the next lifetime. The Latin thinking expressed in *gozar*—that you can be happy right now, just by doing things that feel good—and then also do better in every aspect of life. seems too good to be true. Like that day Ben and Jerry's shops were giving away free ice cream. With sauce and nuts and everything.

But what can I say? Ben and Jerry's Free Cone Day is a thing, and so is the Latin wisdom presented in *gozar*. Use it to give yourself permission to take the time to enjoy simple pleasures. knowing that these are not trivialities, not time-wasting, and not inconvenient distractions. They are the key to your professional, personal, academic, and creative success.

Oh! And then there's the small matter of the fact that simply being happy is all any of us want anyway: the ultimate success and holy grail of achievements.

One last thing: *gozar* is not pretending that suffering doesn't exist. *Gozar* is not a denial of the reality of struggle; it is a refusal to be swallowed by it. *Gozar* is a recognition that suffering and pain coexist with sources of beauty and pleasure, and that you have the freedom to enjoy them. As you do so, you empower yourself to endure and improve your situation. Beginning right now.

How I discovered *gozar*

In our office here at the United Nations Headquarters, we hear the news. Via Crisis Response Unit reports, and bbc.com updates, and code cables from our field presences, we are fully briefed about the unraveling of Venezuela.

What's a code cable, you ask? Good question. A code cable is a letter, really. A communication to the heads of UN peace operations that is carefully drafted, painstakingly edited by about twenty pairs of eyes, and the revised draft re-reviewed by those same eyes (just in case). Then some poor cog in the wheels of bureaucracy (it was me) squeezes through the door of a windowless meeting room somewhere in the bowels of the Secretariat, folds into the wall, edges over to the signatory, and darts across to them with an apologetic grimace and a pen.

With the precious epistle clipped to a folder printed with some combination of olive branches and helmets, I hurry to the third floor of a tower called DC-1, walking with more haste than speed around and around a labyrinth of corridors to . . . OMG, HERE IT IS! BLOODY HELL! RIGHT THEN! A little covered hatch about sixteen-by-sixteen inches.

After an awkward "Hello?" and what felt like forever, the plastic screen covering the hatch slides open, and a woman on the other side reaches for the folder, opens it, nods briefly, and disappears.

Where to?

Well now, I can't be sure, but I imagine her feeding it into a giant prehistoric fax machine, cranking a handle like the arm of a mangle around and around until *CLICK-CLICK-CLICK-CLICK-CLIK-CLICK-WHOOSH! WHIRRRRR! WEEEEEEEEEE- CLONK! SMACK-BRRRRING-BOING-BUBBLE-BLIP-CHIME!* The cable arrives on the desk of a special representative of the Secretary General in Bangui or Baghdad. Just slightly before that moment, somewhere between the *CLICK* of the crank handle and the *WHOOSH* of the cable's descent into a war zone, an email arrives in said representative's inbox.

Say what? You mean . . . after all that hoopla, the communication is sent via email anyway?

Yes. Yes, it is. As an attachment.

So . . . *ummm* . . . what's the p—?"

I will tell you in a bit. But first, where were we?

Oh yes, fretting about Venezuela.

In case you haven't heard, a day in the life of the average Venezuelan involves queuing for hours for food, often to find empty shelves at the end of the line; weeks or even a month without water or electricity; no petrol at all in a country that has the biggest proven oil reserves in the world; and a political pickle involving two governments, three presidents, thousands of armed paramilitaries, and the perpetual threat of a bullet in the chest of anyone who dares to protest. As a humanitarian crisis deepens daily, multimillionaire politicians lord it over impoverished masses who are fearful, fed up, and fleeing in one of the largest migrations of modern times.

Good news! The Peace and Development advisor is visiting from Caracas, so we can get answers to the questions we ask in corridors and queues at the coffee shop.

"Will the military join Guaidó?"

"Will humanitarian relief be held at the border?"

"How can we help the people of Venezuela without propping up an abusive government?"

I walk to the Regional Bureau of Latin America and the Caribbean (RBLAC) in DC-1 for the advisor's briefing. The flags in front of the Secretariat are hardly moving at all in this late summer morning, and are glowing; backlit by the sun shining high in the sky and bouncing off the East River. I arrive a few minutes early, take my seat, and prepare to check email, read the papers in my portfolio, or scroll through the news feed: business as usual.

But this morning is not business as usual. Participants are chatting as they enter—all smiles and a gentle hand on the shoulder, surprised and delighted greetings, kisses and hugs.

"*Holá, Maria! ¿que tal?!*"

"*Que bien de verte!*"

"*¿Cómo estás? Mucho tiempo! ¿Estás bien?*"

I am greeted by the ladies to my left and to my right (both called Maria, and both dazzling in more jewelry, lipstick, and glossy nail polish than I'm used to seeing around here) and by an elegant-looking gentleman with a white beard and nut-brown skin, sitting at the head of the table. He enquires in which bureau I am based, the nature of my work, and my interest in the subject.

Do I work with the Venezuela Country Office?

No, I explain. But my boyfriend is from Venezuela.

"Oh really?!"

As a portly gentleman in a pinstripe suit strides in to sit next to the chair, my new acquaintance announces with delight, "And we have Lucy here from Crisis Bureau!" He gesticulates wildly in my direction as he addresses the group. "And her boyfriend is from . . . VENEZUELA!!!"

He turns back to me with a smile: "and I am from Venezuela, eh!?"

Then back to the meeting: "But I am not her boyfriend *jajajaja!*"

A sort of impromptu Criollo cuisine bingo follows, during which everyone at the table calls out their favorite Venezuelan food.

"Pabellón!"

"Cachapa!"

"Arepa!"

"No, la arepa es Colombiana!" (No, arepas are Colombian!)

"Absolutamente no! Las arepas son Venezolanas!!" (Absolutely not, arepas are Venezuelan!).

"Jajajajaja! No, Colombianos!" (*Heehee!* No, Colombian!).

"Las arepas en Colombia son mas deliciosas!" (The arepas in Colombia are tastier!).

"Jajajjaja! Nunca!!" (Heehee! Never!).

After this culinary merriment, we settle down with a quick tour-de-table. Quick-ish, I should say. Because in a room of Latinos, each with a name more lovely than the last, quick is neither possible nor desirable.

"Maria Gabriela Lucero Garcia de la Parra Martins, Evaluations Office."

"Maria-Jesus Quintero Cardoso Colmenares-Tovar, DPPA."

"Maria Eugenia Cabrera López Bustamente, PBSO."

"Gonzalo Veron Pineda Ramon y Rivera, Regional Bureau."

"Jose Luis Carmelo-Cabre Perez-Rojas, BPPS."

And so it goes, name after name that goes on and on and on and on and on until, finally! A relief for the note-taker: "Jon Evans, Partnerships Bureau."

Formalities observed, we are ready for the presentation: slide after slide of data and analysis detailing the disastrous status quo and its possible development into scenarios that range from a steady worsening of the existing crisis to total collapse of the Bolivarian government; all-out war between supporters of the two governments, and a possible Cold War-style standoff between their global supporters. Discussion followed, identifying what the UN could do in each scenario. No drama, no delusions, no despair. No tutting, brow furrowing, sniffing, or sighing. No stress at all. Just nuts-and-bolts, brass tacks: how can we help Venezuela now?

It occurred to me that a good number of the Marias in the room would be, and surely already were, personally affected by whatever tragedy played out. But if any of them were worried, they were no less warm for it. If they were stressed, well, they were still smiling. And if any of them were fretting, I couldn't tell.

"Just like Alejandro," I mused, on my way back to the office. Never complains. Even though he is unemployed, broke, and responsible for supporting a family of four. Silvia (his sister) is the same. All "Hi! How are you? Oh yes, we are fine here," beaming smiles and sunshine every single time we speak, even though she's probably just spent three hours queuing for a sad-looking lettuce and some corn flour. No tears in RBLAC, either—more like a party. My mind boggled, then got back to Tuesday.

A few weeks later, as cooler weather arrived in New York—all orange trees, crispy leaves, apple cider, and pumpkin spice—Ale went to Venezuela. I wanted to go too. I wanted to see those smiling faces known to me only as pixelated images beaming over WhatsApp; to admire the colossal Angel Falls, the vast Andean mountain range and immense Orinoco Delta; the untouched tropical jungle and dreamlike mist of the cloud forests; the rugged Guiana Highlands and lush Maracaibo Lowlands; the sparkling waters and gleaming sun-kissed sands of the Caribbean coast. With all this ecological bounty, Venezuela is the ideal place to enjoy the beauties of nature.

It is also, alas, the ideal place to be kidnapped. Not safe, Ale reckoned, for me to visit the (statistically proven) "most violent city in the world" that he calls home. The *favela* (slum) that he comes from, La Vega, was notoriously dangerous even during the oil-boom-easy-money-good-time years. So off he went solo, dragging a suitcase packed full of everything from tuna cans to bottles of vitamins, misshapen and marked with a fluorescent orange "HEAVY" sticker.

I waved him off at the airport; watching as he went through security, past the recombobulation area, and disappeared from view.

Then nothing.

No phone call. No message. No email. Nothing.

Not a sausage.

Was he still in transit through Trinidad? Did he arrive in Caracas? Did he get through the airport okay, with passport still in hand? Or was his name on some sort of list? Did he get to La Vega? Did he lose his phone? Was it stolen? Or was there just no electricity or internet? Let me check; did all the Caribbean airlines flights depart from Port of Spain?

Well I needn't have worried because they were having a gay old time. An incoming video call revealed the family upside-down, all smiles. Someone giggled, put down a drink, and set the phone right-side up. And there they all were—faces I recognized, and many more I did not: rosy-cheeked and grinning ear-to-ear as two people danced in the background, one-half of them in view, stepping and swirling to Celia Cruz.

After enthusiastic *"Holas,"* grinning and waving, and thanks for the gifts I had sent along in the stuffed suitcase, I had a quick chat with Ale alone. We were no longer on video (trying to save the burden on a limited bandwidth) but I could tell he was cock-a-hoop. "It's great, love! Everyone is here! Cousins, Aunty, Uncle, Grandma. So nice love! Fabi (his nephew) says it is the best time of his life, *jajajajajaja!*"

And then I heard about the many "so nice" things: a feast his mother saved up from the government food box; Fabi (not a small child, or even a particularly young one) insisting on sleeping with Uncle Alejo; logistical gymnastics to get a car and petrol to drive to Choroní tomorrow, a beach town on the other side of a forested mountain range.

And that was that. Slightly confused, but certainly contented, I went about my days, which at some point included a coffee with a colleague. We hadn't met many times before, but were about the same age, got on well, and found it easy to work together. As we were wrapping up, she asked where I was from, and I asked the same. "Venezuela?! Oh!"

I explained the link, "He's there now actually."

I asked the server for the bill, which in this café is quite a project, and remarked, "You know, it's the funniest thing, but for all you hear about the chaos there, they're having the best time ever, it seems. Seriously! They've pulled off some sort of minor miracle to get a car and fuel to hang out on the beach in Choroní! Have you been to Choroní? It looks like it's made up! Like a cartoon tropical beach! Absolute heaven!"

"Ah, yes," she replied, smiling slightly; eyes sparkling "*Se sufre pero se goza,* no?"

She looked at my blank face. "You don't know it? *Se sufre pero se goza!*' (one suffers, but enjoys). It's a Venezuelan phrase: like no matter what is going on, with politics or job or family or whatever, you can say, "Come on, let's have a drink! Or go to the beach, listen to music, have a dance, go for a walk, do something nice; something that makes you feel good no matter what is happening all around."

Se sufre pero se goza. You suffer, but enjoy.

"There is even a book about it; a Venezuelan journalist wrote it. Laureano Marquez Perez. And a song too."

Smiling, savoring my latest linguistic treasure, I put my card back in my wallet. "So that's what they're doing! *Se sufre pero se goza!* Suffering but enjoying; suffering; suffering but having a good time anyway."

I ordered the book. I listened to the song. But all I really needed to know was revealed in that conference room in Midtown Manhattan, and pixelated images from La Vega. Not wealthy people, you understand, Ale's family has no government affiliation, special privileges, or advantages. They suffer dictatorship, deprivation, insecurity, and injustice just the same as everyone else in the slum. They suffer. But they also enjoy. All hell is breaking loose, and they enjoy themselves all the while, by doing simple things that make them feel good. Small, simple things that give comfort and strength, and make it possible—pleasurable even—to endure and overcome the daily struggles of life in these circumstances. This is how they live *se sufre pero se goza*, suffer but enjoy, and say yes to life, in spite of everything.

Gozar (Spanish): to have fun, to enjoy, to have a good time, to get a kick out of something, to take delight. It can also mean "to seduce." You get the picture. *Gozar* is whatever you do to put you in a tiki party frame of mind, even when the political, personal, professional, equivalent of hailstones and rain and slate and scrubbing brushes are hammering against your side, swept down from the heavens and rooftops by a harsh wind that makes any onward progress seem impossible. It could be remembering a loved one. It could be reflecting that "this too shall pass." It could be anticipating a nice moment to come. Finding just one good quality or opportunity in a challenging person or situation. Reading a poem or writing a note to a pal, looking at a pleasant scene or pretty object, listening to good music, watching a funny video, playing a game, taking a bath, seeing the sky, the sunrise, the sunset, a single shard of light, admiring a purple wildflower poking through cracked concrete, dancing for five minutes on your kitchen floor, or gyrating in the small space between your bed and the window and the wall, drinks with a buddy, baking, bobbing about in the ocean, sipping cocktails around and around your eyes with pink drinking glasses, roller skating, or going really fast on your electric scooter around and around and around and around the lake until your coat whips up around you like a cape. Anything at all. Anything at all that makes you feel like it's a zippidee-doodah day; that is *gozar*, baby.

Very important: *gozar* is not just hedonistic arsing about. It's serious business. These two things are true: 1) The *gozo*—joy, comfort, strength, and calm you get from simple, pleasurable things—makes you feel good. 2) That good feeling state unlocks your intelligence, ingenuity, creativity, and capabilities of every kind, so that you not only feel better, but actually do better, in every aspect of your life. As Alejandro's family knows, *gozar* makes it easier to get through the day, by activating the physical, mental, and emotional strength they need to bring to the daily challenges of life in suboptimal circumstances—from obtaining medicine to finding a way to earn a bit of money.

But fair enough, you've never met them, and you don't know much about life under dictatorship. So let me share some statistics to demonstrate what folks have discovered in the slum, and also in research from the universities of Harvard, Cambridge, Stanford, Sydney, Princeton, Yale, Berkeley, LSE, Milan and Melbourne, Cornell and Columbia. According to Harvard positive psychology enthusiast Shawn Achor in his book, *The Happiness Advantage*, when your brain is happy, it "performs significantly better than it does when negative, neutral or stressed." Your intelligence rises, your creativity rises, your energy levels rise, and these areas of your life improve: your marriage, social life, altruism, learning, cognition, productivity (including efficiency, speed, and accuracy), job satisfaction, pay grade, performance evaluations, managerial competence, health (including immunity, blood pressure, pain, sleep, life expectancy, and vision).

These are the key conclusions of hundreds of studies, involving hundreds of thousands of people. They prove that whoever told you that you'll be happy only if you put your nose to the grindstone and pump out enough achievements, was wrong. Decline the social engagements, cancel the dance class, and battle the urge to take a break, and you actually slow yourself down. Time to rethink "distractions": the people who take the time for such seemingly trivial things are 31 percent more productive, have 37 percent better sales figures, and do better in every aspect of life. So great are the real-world rewards of happiness that Achor calls a positive and engaged brain "the greatest competitive advantage in our modern economy."[4]

His recommendation? *Gozar.* Do simple things that make you feel good. Take that break. Go for a walk. Reach out to a friend. Say something nice to someone. Think, write, speak of things (happy moments past; things you are grateful for now) that make you feel good. Our brains are like single processors: they can only do one thing at a time. So when you are absorbed in something that feels good, you place yourself in a sort of "bubble of positivity" that protects you from the negative effects of whatever political, personal, or professional storm is brewing. It is a peaceful zone of contentment in which you can rest and reenergize, and from which you can re-emerge stronger, happier, and better able to deal with the challenges you face.

---

4. *The Happiness Advantage: How a Positive Brain Fuels Success in Work and Life*, Achor; Currency Press (New York, 2010).

So there we have it: *gozar*. Venezuelan wisdom validated by science.

Interesting, right?

Well, strap yourself in, because it's about to get even more interesting. Much of this "positive psychology" research is based on the professional practice, academic work, and lived experience of renowned psychiatrist and neurologist, Viktor Frankl, MD, PhD, who spent three years' detention in concentration camps during the Second World War. Intense deprivation in the camps claimed the lives of Dr. Frankl's wife, father, mother, and brother—and very nearly killed him too. But Dr. Frankl lived. And he discovered a few things about how to live. Namely, that *gozar* is essential to a good life. *Gozar*, he discovered, enabled an inmate to have a "rich inner life in a context of physical and mental deprivation." And this rich inner life helped the person to survive. The inmates who made the effort to *gozar* were the ones who found the strength (physical, mental, emotional) to survive and overcome the dehumanizing effects of their surroundings; becoming brave, dignified, and unselfish, creative, compassionate, and kind, even in the context of intense abuse. "To discover that there was any semblance of art in a concentration camp must be surprise enough for an outsider, but he may be even more astonished to hear that one could find a sense of humor there as well," Frankl wrote in his best-selling book, *Man's Search for Meaning*.[5]

He described how enjoying simple acts like telling jokes, singing, storytelling, poetry, makeshift cabaret,

---

5. *Man's Search for Meaning* by Victor E. Frankl (trans. Lasch); Beacon Press (Boston, 2006).

nature, memories of loved ones, imagined future comforts or comical events, or acts of kindness (offering a last piece of bread, volunteering to care for fellow inmates with infectious diseases) were "the soul's weapon in the fight for self-preservation." These were not frivolous acts, or insensitive ones. They were the sources of comfort and strength that enabled inmates to physically survive, and spiritually "rise above" the intense suffering in the camps. Through observing the possibility for, and effect of, *gozar*, even in the context of the humanitarian catastrophe that was Auschwitz, Theresienstadt, Kaufering, Buchenwald, and Türkheim, Frankl concluded: "Everything can be taken from a man but one thing: the last of the human freedoms—to choose one's attitude in any given set of circumstances, to choose one's own way."

Gozar is application of that human freedom to the challenge of finding sources of enjoyment, no matter what circumstances you find yourself in.

Or not. Freedom is just that: choice. To choose to delight in pleasure and beauty, or to despair over pain and ugliness. After all, you'll always get those people who will say, "Oh wow! A field of sunshine!" as they gaze with delight upon acres of daisies, buttercups, and candy floss clouds. Bright sunlight beaming onto a meadow in full bloom; butterflies fluttering, bees buzzing while lush grass sways slightly in a gentle breeze. And by their side, surveying the same scene, someone else who says, "Yes, but there's a shadow under that tree." And rustling about her toes in the long grass . . . "Look! A rusty old Coke can!"

Gotcha. I've met that person. But what's all this got to do with a code cable?

Ah! Well now. It seems to me that in this age of the internet, using a code cable to communicate hinders success. Better to upgrade to email: a simple, proven strategy for success at work.

And now that we know that *gozar* improves all aspects of our existence, better to upgrade to this simple, proven strategy for more success in life, no? Why labor under the traditional Western illusion that we'll be happy only if we focus-focus-focus and work-work-work to achieve our goals, when we have evidence to show that this approach actually slows us down and undermines achievement? And why turn away from the world, toward the "inner realm" of traditional Eastern thought, when it's clear that we'll have to wait many years for meditation to change our brains in a way that promotes happiness? Unless you're willing to wait for quite some time to have the success and happiness you seek (possibly after retirement or rebirth as a Latino), you might as well Latin yourself up right now with *gozar*: a simple, proven approach to success in all its forms. Do small, simple things that help you feel good. Do small simple things that make you feel good, especially when you don't.

And sometimes you won't. Because life—as you know from hip hop sage Run-D.M.C.—is like that. And that's the way it is. If you feel awful one day, don't worry. There's nothing wrong with you. There's nothing wrong with life either. It's just doing its thing: throwing sources of struggle in your general direction, and inviting you to *gozar,* so that you can overcome them and create those moments of joy which, let's face it, may well matter more in the end than any of your academic or artistic credentials, professional accomplishments, and bank balance.

But who knows, really, what matters most in the end? We'll know when we get there. Right here, right now, we are in our struggle of one degree or another. And it's just nice to know, isn't it? That for all life causes us to suffer, it also enables us to enjoy. You, me, and the people you are most worried about; every single one of us can enjoy. And in enjoying: feel better, do better, have more, get more done, endure, overcome, and enjoy every one of those achievements made possible by feeling good, and made all the sweeter through lack and longing. Such is the mystery and the magic in our mean and miserable and marvelous world. Life may be unfair, but not so unfair that we can't be happy anyway. Life may be cruel, but not so cruel that the people who suffer the most cannot have a successful life anyway; a happy one.

So maybe in a funny sort of way, my dear reader, life is fair. So fair that every one of us has what we need to be happy anyway: freedom. Maybe in a funny sort of way, life is kind: so kind that just by doing simple things right now, you, me, and the people who have the least can feel good and do better. I don't know if this is the "light upon light!" spoken of in mystical Middle Eastern teachings, but I do know this: life is good. Life is so good, that you—all of us—can *se sufre pero se goza*.

This word comes to you from Venezuela, with love. With love and in the hope that you use it to become the empowered and energized, creative and capable person who can endure and overcome all things with grace and good cheer. With grace, good cheer, and (YES! That's the spirit!) maybe even a strut, a shimmy, and a smile.

I leave you with the words of the mighty Socrates: "Enjoy yourself; it's later than you think." And more important than you may realize.

"I think I am in my last days, but it doesn't really matter because I have had such a beautiful life. I have lived through many wars and have lost everything many times—including my husband, my mother, and my beloved son. Yet life is beautiful, and I have so much to learn and enjoy. I have no space nor time for pessimism and hate. Life is beautiful, love is beautiful, nature and music are beautiful. Everything we experience is a gift, a present we should cherish and pass on to those we love." —Alice Herz-Sommer, pianist and concentration camp survivor, who died at age 110 years.

7

Alhamdulillah

هَٱلْحَمْدُ لِلَّٰه - **Alhamdulillah** (excl)

Pronunciation: ȯl-ˈhəmˈduˌ lēˈle (al-Ham-doo-Lee-leh).

Origin: Arabic (Middle East).

Definition: Literal meaning: "Praise be to God" or "Thanks to God." An expression of gratitude uttered in the midst of misfortune, in anticipation of benefit from that misfortune. An exclamation acknowledging the goodness in all things—even undesirable experiences. Expresses an expectation that all situations serve you in some way, giving rise to something for which you will be grateful.

How to use *alhamdulillah*

GOOD NEWS! There's a word we can use to feel comfortable, even in uncomfortable situations. A word to help find a reason to be happy, even in the most irritating circumstances—and even if you have to scrape the bottom of the barrel of blessings to see it there, glinting in the light of your conviction that it exists, and determination to find it.

91

A word to say when you're freaking out, to help you return to a peaceful and productive state.

The word is *alhamdilullah:* a linguistic superhero that rips its shirt off and runs to the rescue while you're stuck in a stressful situation. *KABOOM! POW! ZAP! ALHAMDULILLAH!* Maybe you missed an accident because you missed that plane. Or maybe you had time to read a book, or meet someone interesting, or learn patience, or pick up some perfume at the duty free. And if not? Ah well, at least you're not dead.

You've heard of the benefits of gratitude: reduced pain, anxiety, inflammation, blood sugar, and blood pressure. Gratitude leads the brain to produce the same neurotransmitters that you get from listening to good music, hugging, gambling, a massage, chocolate, run, promotion, pay raise, or that moment when *zippadeedoodah! zippadeeday!* you reach a mighty ten stamps on your loyalty card and this coffee is free. Even simply listing a few things you are grateful for four times a week reduces stress and increases happiness. Imagine the benefits of expressing gratitude throughout the day by punctuating your paragraphs with a word that expresses an expectation that all things serve you?

Brain health expert, Dr. P. Murali Doraiswamy, hypothesized that "if [thankfulness] were a drug, it would be the world's best-selling product with a health maintenance indication for every major organ system."[6] Distinguished friends,

---

6. Stillness in the Storm: An Agent of Conscious Evolution. (December 2, 2014) "The Science and Practice of Gratitude," Justin Deschamps. https://stillnessinthestorm .com/2014/12/the-science-and-practice-of-gratitude/

esteemed reader, ladies and gentlemen, it gives me great pleasure to present *alhamdilullah:* free linguistic medicine for all of humanity, from the Arabic speaking people of the world with love.

مرحبا بك. You're welcome!

How I discovered *alhamdulillah*

It was a really hot day. The kind of hot that makes people crazy and dogs die. In the setting sun, the car felt like a furnace. "Can we open the window please, Ayman?"

Zzzzzzz

In flowed fumes from the traffic jam we had just entered, along with the roar of protesters in Tahrir Square, like a football crowd in the distance. Actually, can we close the window please, Ayman?"

"I sorry. AC brok-id."

"No worries, Ayman."

Quite a lot was broken in Egypt now, and even the ever-cheerful Ayman seemed stressed. Few tourists meant few clients, and petrol was hard to get. The new government was sending supplies to Gaza—a nice gesture, but the resulting queues outside petrol stations were becoming unbearable. Black market supplies were often cut with water, causing cars to break down and traffic jams throughout the city. As we joined yet another, I sighed heavily. And Ayman once again said, "*Alhamdulillah!*"

"Ayman, what does *alhamdulillah* mean?"

"*Ahhhmmm* . . . thanks God."

"Yes, but you say *alhamdulillah* even when bad things happen—like this traffic."

"Yes. Thanks God for this small problem. Not big problem."

"Well, what if there is a big problem?"

He raised his hands enthusiastically, and turned back to face me with a gap-toothed grin. "Thanks God for big problem *yanni* ... it—*ehhhh* make better somehow ... Good thing come."

I raised my eyebrows and sat back, taking a swig of water from a plastic bottle so thin that it cracked and popped under the pressure of my fingertips.

And there it was. Right there in the window, the good thing. A spectacular sunset: a huge red sun casting a soft warm light on everything as the call to prayer began. Orange sellers chatting in the sunshine; keffiyah-turbaned men squatting around a shisha balanced on a red plastic crate, passing the pipe between them as children played, wiggling and giggling at each other. Large men in abeyas bobbed about atop tiny trotting donkeys, waving to neighbors out buying bread.

Alhamdulillah for this traffic jam-wrapped gift: the opportunity to enjoy a moment of peace and beauty in a stressed and chaotic city. *Alhamdulillah* for this benefit of misfortune. *Alhamdulillah* for the problem creating a good thing.

Isn't that how it goes? You miss the train. The next one isn't for seven whole minutes. "Seven minutes?! SEVEN MINUTES?! This isn't the suburbs!" Then as if to punish you for disrespecting the L, no train at all. Just an ear-piercing screech followed by an indiscernible mumble over a crackling tannoy. Something about "signal failures." *Sigh.* A platform of pissed-off people squeezes up the steps to the street to hail a cab or curse in the queue at the bus stop. *Slim pickings for lunch*, you think to yourself as you eyeball the meter, ticking along too quickly this far from pay day.

The pipes burst in the flat upstairs and you wake to find a dome-shaped hump protruding into your kitchen. A big chunk of plaster crashes to the floor past your ears. *BAM!* just as you go to get a spoon for your cereal. Within twenty-four hours, you half expect to see an ark float into the bathroom as you look on like the poor chap in Edvard Munch's "The Scream."

You show up late to the meeting that was rescheduled three times—only notification about the final change wasn't forwarded to you. Standing in front of the frosted glass, observing an event in full flow, you wonder which is worse: being framed in the doorway of a crowded room before squeezing past forty knees, sending papers and coffee cups flying as you edge toward the single seat left on the other side of the room, or scuttling back to your desk, head down, papers in hand?

You can't get on your flight because "Yeah, I can see your reservation. But it's not been ticketed, I'm afraid."

"Yes, I know you've got an e-ticket, but it's not showing in the system. So I can't let you on, you see."

You say something like: "Right, okay, so how do you suggest I get to London by 10.45?" but in your head you all "ARE YOU #$%&*!! KIDDING ME?!"

The virulent expletives. The vigorous eye-rolling. The tutting. All of it is justified. So too the head-shaking and nostril flaring and jaw clenching and little vein popping in the side of your skull, like something from *Where the Wild Things Are.* Let the wild rumpus begin: the righteous rage, the stress, and almost any way you soothe it are totally understandable, and absolutely fine.

Just . . . unnecessary. Let the wild rumpus pause while we stop to ask, "What would Ayman do?"

Say, "*Alhamdulillah*." Thank you in anticipation of a positive outcome even of this sorry state of affairs. Ask how this situation (yes, even this flipping awful situation) serves him. Expect an advantage from this miserable misfortune, and invite it to reveal itself. Yep. While the rest of us are cursing the MTA and management company and colleague ("Who reschedules a meeting three times FFS?!") and Opodo, and ourselves for being (insert insult here), Ayman is kicking back in his Nissan with Oum Kalthoum and a bottle of water, reflecting on how marvelous it is that all things serve you, and waiting for a blessing.

"*Alhamdulillah* for this (small/medium/giant/massive flipping) problem, *yanni* (good thing come)."

Alhamdulillah that you missed the plane. *Alhamdulillah* for the extra time to finish a few things and sleep off that unbecoming look: like a one-eyed monster, wandering about and wondering *Where's the Starbucks?*

Alhamdulillah that you didn't get the train you wanted to get. *Alhamdulillah* that you weren't stuck in a tunnel for three hours while MTA mended the signals. *Alhamdulillah* for the chance to zip over the Brooklyn Bridge, watching the light bounce off the East River, high above the cattle-crowds in the dusty and decrepit subway.

Alhamdulillah that your flat got flooded. *Alhamdulillah* for redecorating on the insurance company's dime . . . *ahhhhh* . . . this sofa's really rather lovely, isn't it?

Alhamdulillah that you missed the meeting. *Alhamdulillah* that you got all the information you needed anyway, plus a nice coffee and chat with the colleague who did attend, and an extra hour to complete an urgent brief. Cherry-cherry-cherry JACKPOT!

And yet, part of you doubts. Part of you doubts that life really can be that good. And that part has lots of reasons. So let's give it the floor, shall we? On your feet, friend!

"Thank you, Pollyanna, that was very nice." But what about bad things? Really bad things? Serious struggles. Big ticket bummers like, oh, I dunno, loss of a loved one. War, even. The Holocaust. Break-ups. Being too embarrassed to invite your friends over because your home very much does not look like a Pinterest picture. Having your card declined while people queue behind you at the check-out and you turn out your pockets to find . . . yup. As suspected: not going to cover it.

Okay. War, the Holocaust, break-ups, dismal dwellings, debt, and death. That it?

Yep. That's it. All of those things. Really challenging moments. Moments when it feels like the whole world is caving in. Moments when everything seems pointless except perhaps staying in bed forever with a large quantity of ice-cream, a big spoon, and a bottle of Jim Beam.

Absolutely. I get it. A few questions for you first though, if you don't mind. Didn't war lead to historic achievements like women's right to vote? Didn't the Holocaust lead to 100 years of peace in Europe, the United Nations, and global improvements in peace and progress of every kind, from tele-communications to life-expectancy? Didn't that experience of suffering burn into the mind an awareness that ordinary people bleed too, and on their sacrifice depends all that we value? Didn't it bring us the human rights movement and systems to take them forward—albeit imperfectly? Didn't

COVID-19 help to heal the environment in some way, and awaken a yearning for justice, and provoke countless acts of kindness, neighbor-to-neighbor? And isn't it true that love never dies? And nor does the happiness of shared moments, or the value of wisdom learned, or the comfort of standing together at a time of loss, in solidarity and the shared realization that each day is precious, the time to live fully is now, and that this experience of standing with and for one other is the only thing that really matters?

What if you could say *alhamdullilah* for all of it: every single thing you wouldn't have chosen? What if they built your compassion and increased your capacity to love? What if they taught you how important it is to be kind? What if they helped you to feel with other people in pain, and made you more willing and able to do something positive for them? What if they gave you information about what you want, or stripped away what was stopping you from going after it: the dead-end job, the lifeless relationship, the stuff you don't need, the complacency, the unhelpful habits of thought, and word, and deed? What if even in those moments when you feel further from being who you want to be, and having what you want to have, you were actually closer to it? What if *alhamdulillah* encapsulates a truth discovered through thousands of years of lived experience, and proven again and again and again: all things serve you? Then . . . you might as well be grateful, no? Grateful for everything.

Still not convinced? Alright then. Forget the "everything serves you" thing. Be grateful only because it helps you feel better. And when you feel better, you do better. *Alhamdullilah* for that. And *alhamdullilah* for a word that gives access to a state of grace, in situations of struggle large and small. A word that helps you to see the world in a new way. A way that reveals its beauty and blessings; giving you the strength to become the version of yourself who can endure and overcome all things with grace and good cheer.

You don't have to, obviously. You can be as graceful or grim as you want to be; as cheery or cheesed off as you choose. Freedom, eh? It's a fine thing. And you are absolutely free to curse and weep and moan and wail and howl and blame and shame yourself or anyone else for any number of things, forever. Free to live in that place—one might say hell—created by those thoughts and the feelings they elicit. You can climb into bed, right down under the covers with your bourbon and your Ben & Jerry's, and stay there—oh, forever, probably—surrounded by tissues and takeaway containers and smelly socks. OR . . . or you can open the curtains. Let the light in. Squint in that light, pick up your socks, put them in the laundry. Listen to that voicemail you've been ignoring. Get back to it.

Move forward. Endure, overcome, move through. Not one day at a time or one hour at a time, but one choice at a time. The choice is this: to find one small thing to be grateful for.

Alhamdulillah that I only have to get through today.

Alhamdullilah that change is the fundamental fact of nature, and this too shall pass.

Alhamdulillah now I come to think of it that this pillow has the perfect amount of puff—not too much, not too little.

Alhamdulillah that that book there on the bedside table is quite good.

Alhamdullilah that I've got those nice yoghurts in the fridge. Ah, what the heck. I think I'll have one now. I deserve it. And even if I don't deserve it, I'm just going to go ahead and have it because I get to decide how my life goes, at least to some degree.

Alhamdulillah that tomorrow is a new day. Friday, in fact. Good.

Alhamdulillah. You see how it works? In that simple choice—to find just one thing to be grateful for—is a shift of mood that makes you feel better, and a shift of energy that gives you strength to move forward. Both bring you closer to that place of peace, of easy happiness, where you want to be. And in that feeling of appreciation for something pleasant, something beautiful, something heart-warming, something comforting, something good, can you really say that you are not already there? In the good-feeling place that you want to be?

What's that? Can't find anything to be grateful for? Nothing at all? Not a problem. Just think of someone who's even worse off you than you, and be glad you're not them. Think of a situation that's even worse than the one you're in now, and say, "*Alhamdillulah!*" for your lesser suffering.

As Dr. Seuss put it: when things get bad, remember that some people have it worse.[7] Like the folks working on the Bungebung Bridge across Boober Bay at Bumm Ridge. Think your job's bad? Theirs is worse. Don't like your nose? Consider the Schlottz: the Crumple-horn, web-footed, green-bearded Schlottz, whose tail is entailed with unsolvable knots. Crummy apartment? Well suppose that you lived in that forest in France, where the average young person just hasn't a chance to escape from the perilous pants-eating-plants! But

---

7. *Did I Ever Tell You How Lucky You Are?* by Dr. Seuss. RandomHouse, New York, 1973.

your pants are safe! You're a fortunate guy. And you ought to be shouting how lucky am I!?

How lucky are you!?

Alright, I get it—not as lucky as you want to be. But hold on, my dear. HOLD ON. You're going to get luckier. You're going to move on up, my love, one *alhamdulillah* at a time. I promise.

––––––

"Let us rise up and be thankful, for if we didn't learn a lot today, at least we learned a little, and if we didn't learn a little, at least we didn't get sick, and if we got sick, at least we didn't die."

—Leo Buscaglia

8

Mudita

मुदिता **Mudita** (verb)

Pronunciation: moo-dee-ta (mūdēʹta).

Origin: Sanskrit (Indian sub-continent) and Pali, with no English counterpart.

Definition: Vicarious pleasure in another person's happiness. Sympathetic or unselfish joy in the good fortune of others.

How to use *mudita*

Ever wondered why billionaires like Bill Gates and Zell Kravinsky are more excited about giving money and organs away than hanging out in a hot tub in Aspen? Turns out that giving time or money to another person or cause makes you happier, healthier, and richer.

Sounds mad, doesn't it? Perhaps because we're stuck with the ye olde idea that nice guys finish last, and that helping others is for charities and suckers—or wealthy people who can claim it as a tax break, or score "social good" points with consumers. But what can I tell you? The benefits of being kind are proven. They include a feeling of well-being known as the "helpers' high," bigger earnings, improved physical and mental health, a sense that you have more time, and greater satisfaction from the money you spend.

Ancient sages knew what modern science now proves, and they summed it up in the word *mudita,* meaning vicarious pleasure in another person's happiness. You can use this Sanskrit word to motivate yourself to do good, and feel better.

How I discovered *mudita*

On balance, I'd give my time in Nepal a B-minus. On the one hand, I got sick and nearly died. On the other hand, I learned a lot. But before the passing of time that allowed for this balanced view, I would have given it a Z. Or is F the worst grade? In which case, F. You get my meaning: when departure day came, I was eager to leave.

Eager, eager, eager. Like both arms up skyward. "Okay! Take me away! Had enough now! Thanks!" But with jetpacks and teleportation still some way off, I had to go to the airport. No biggie: pack up and get out. Right?

Ahhhhh . . . no. No-no. Like much else during my time in Nepal, trying to leave was . . . trying.

Could I get a taxi? Could I get any transport to the airport? No. No-no. On the day of my departure, protests (*bandha*) brought the country to a standstill again, and there was, quite literally, no transport. Drivers were at risk of being pelted with stones, having their vehicles set on fire, or bricks thrown at them. So the streets were empty but for stray dogs sleepily snapping at flies in the intense afternoon sun, and me: standing on the dusty red lane in front of Mrs. Pradhan's house in my red dress with my red suitcase, red-faced and damp with sweat. I probably looked like I'd been boiled. Not that anybody could see me of course. Everyone was either protesting in front of the Constitutional Assembly, hitting passers-by with sticks, or sitting it out at home.

With just an hour left before my flight, I was at my wit's end. To the extent that I could think at all in this exhausted, exasperated, emaciated state, I wondered why a country that clearly never wanted me here—"*Bideshi!*" (foreigner!) "*Khoire!*" (white person!)—wouldn't just LET ME LEAVE!? Hand on hips, huffing and puffing and sweating and swatting bugs away, this was a low.

Then, a sound.

A sound like wheels on small stones, but might as well have been coronation trumpets. Then a vision. A vision of a vehicle at the corner. A tiny, ancient, van like an upturned bread bin appearing at the corner and wobbling up the lane. It might as well have been a Batmobile; I went cock-a-hoop. *Oh! Oh oh oh oh oh oh oh!* A beacon of hope! A beacon of hope in the form of an extremely tiny van!

I flailed my arms about madly.

The small, wiry man in a *topi* (colorful Nepali hat) behind the wheel looked startled. He stared at me, wide-eyes unblinking, mouth open. *Oh oh oh oh oh oh oh! Why is this red-faced, wild-eyed woman waving her arms about at me?!* These were, I imagined, his thoughts as he *ummd* and *ahhed* about what to do: *On the one hand, she's a khoire, so probably not involved in the bandha. On the other hand, she's clearly a hot mess of anger and anxiety same as everyone else on the streets today, and my strategy was to avoid every one of them. Oh bloody hell . . . .*

He slows to a stop in front of me, reaches into a doorless glove compartment, pulls out a loose handle, attaches it to the door, and winds down the window. An excruciating delay.

In breathless, broken Nepali, I blurt out too many details about my sweaty, stressful situation, and ask him will he pleasepleasepleasepleasepleaseplease OMG, please take me to the airport?

He waggles his head "no," which in Nepal means "yes," and in a red-hot minute, WE'RE OFF!!

The van, unused to going at any speed much faster than a carnival float, lurches forward, sending the red suitcase smashing straight into the back of my seat. BAM! With the sound of some broken bits squealing, we hurtle through passageways and side-streets and teeter dangerously close to the edge of the Bagmati River. Wooden prayer beads tied to the rearview mirror swing sharply from side-to-side. The terrified driver prays over and over and over: *please God do not let the protestors set my van on fire today; please God that we have enough fuel; please God that the van does not break down now.* He mutters himself into a trance, bobbing back and forth in the seat.

This prayer-induced swaying causes the ancient and unroadworthy vehicle to lurch unsteadily around corners and piles of rubbish as we bounce along potholed paths, narrowly missing four separate cows, two *stupas* (shrines), and a bearded *sadhu* (holy man) in a long white robe, sipping a milkshake.

Just as I wonder whether this last trip through Kathmandu might actually be the last trip of my life, I notice a solar-powered prayer wheel spinning on the dashboard. Next to it, a small white and gold and orange plastic Ganesh holds up a friendly palm. And from a peeling, metallic sticker on the steering wheel, Babaji the Afro-haired Holy man smiles hopefully.

AHHHHHH! RIGHT! FINALLY! THE AIRPORT! THE AIRPORT! I jump out of the van, grab my suitcase, and pull out all the money I have: about $100 in rupees. Enough to feed this kind man's family for weeks. But he will not accept it. He waggles his head in the specific way that means "no," places his hands in front of his face, bows his head, and smiles.

I try again, insisting.

This time, he waggles both his hand and his head in a more firm "no," and smiles. Smiles, it seems, with every cell in his body. That's right. This man whom I have inconvenienced, stressed, and cost time, money, and perhaps even lifespan, is grinning ear-to-ear, shining tongue behind brown teeth, eyes sparkling, delighted.

I made the plane.

The bigger miracle, I thought to myself as we flew over the majestic Himalaya, was the driver's delight. Why was he delighted and determined not to take a *paisa* from me, when I had surely been a burden to him? No one risks the real danger of driving during a *bandha* unless they can't afford not to. Why did he not accept cash that he surely needed? As we passed through vertical clouds like a mystical mountain range of huge, ethereal puffs and swirls soaring high to the heavens, I pondered this mystery and ate mini packets of pretzels.

I found the answer six months and two weeks later, in the Pretzel Capital of the World: USA. Specifically, in a barn in way-out West Texas. A barn that smelled earthy like leather and iron and rust, grain and hay and feed, in the middle of a vast expanse of sand and sky. An old barn made oddly beautiful by stillness and perhaps also the reading of scripture. For this, my dear reader, ain't no ordinary barn. This is Cowboy Church.

10:00 a.m: Still early for some, and sleepy eyes squint slowly in the softly sobering sunshine of the Sunday morning light. It slices through windows up high, forming clear golden shards. Flecks of dust and dander sparkle as they turn in those rays, glinting and glistening like tiny stars in the sunlight as soft swirls of cigarette smoke twist up from cool darkness. Watching them is simple entertainment as we sit in red plastic chairs with metal frames, smoking. Smokin' and dippin' in Stetsons and square-toe boots and jeans worn for days and smelling of diesel and cowpats.

Except for me. I am smelling slightly of sweat and sunscreen probably, in a denim dress that is no one's idea of Sunday best. Here at Cowboy Church, all are welcome to be as they are—high or hungover or wearing yesterday's socks. No hymns; just nice country classics. No footnoted philosophical musings or theatrical threats of fire and brimstone, just a simple sermon from a lay preacher in blue jeans, leather belt with a big silver buckle, brown boots, and a blue-and-green checked shirt. He stands at the front of the barn. No platform, no lectern, no cassock. He looked just like the rest of us, standing at the same level as the rest of us. Only he was slightly front and center and standing, about to preach:

"I wan' tell y'all about a calf at the feed trough that got choked," he began.

"I mean, he was literally backin' up. An' I couldn't figure out why he was backing up, but he'd gotten a big ole wad of feed in his mouth, I mean a BIG old bite. An' he tried to swallow it all at once, and that wad, it hung. It hung, so he was backin' up away from that pressure. An' every now an' then he'd kinda stick his ole neck out an' he's even . . ."

The preacher started gurning and stretching out his face and arms and neck to mimic the troubled cow. "An' I thought— well! He's fit to have an epileptic fit an' fall over right here, you know? He's fit to rack out."

The preacher started to pace about in the small space at the front. "An' Jay Lawson sent me a message and said, 'I bet he's choking.' An' so we talked about one of the reasons we choke is for trough space, when we feel like, 'I'm not going to get my bite.' 'An there ain't gonna be enough feed, but I'm hungry, and I gotta . . ." the preacher motions pushing, shoving, jostling.

"An so sometimes you take it too aggressive, or you take too much at one time, an' you swallow too fast. An' in our spiritual journey, we gotta make room for others at the trough. Gotta make room for others. Y'all gotta trust that you're gonna get what you need, and make room for others at the trough."

He looked at us with conviction, locking a few eyes.

"Gotta make room for others," he repeated, turning to the left and pacing. "Y'all gotta share. Because y'all ain't gonna feel good if you keep all God's blessin's for yourself. If you don't share the strength of your heart, of your mind, of your spirit, if you just keep all them blessin's for yourself, ain't gonna feel good, you git me? Gonna get sick, gonna feel bad. So, you gotta share. And when you do, you git more blessin's—like as if you just upgraded your dinner from a hamburger to a sixteen-ounce steak. BOO-YA!"

A gentleman smoking next to me in a Stetson looked up, and smirked.

"Now," the preacher goes on, "an' this is really important. All y'all need to hear this." He stopped pacing and perched on a little stack of haybales at the front and center, steel toes touching a poured concrete floor worn rough by a thousand hooves.

"Aint none a y'all gonna find a cure for cancer." He seemed to be looking directly at me.

"Ain't no one here gonna send a rocket to space." He gets up to start pacing again.

"Hell most of us ain't never even been to New Mexico. And that's alright. God don't mind. Don't mind at all. But folks all a'y'all can greet the check-out girl real nice at Food King. You can put yer cart back when yer done. Ye'kin let somebody go ahead a you in line. Ye'kin call the folks from time to time—don't cost you nothin'. Call in on yer neighbor; say howdy, sumthin' real nice 'bout the day. Take 'em sumthin' to eat if they ain't feeling right. Ain't gotta make a big performance out of it. Don't need no education or million bucks or fancy get-up to make our world better. Hell, you ain't even got to clean your boots."

Then we sang, "Drop Kick Me Jesus Through the Goalposts of Life," and left. Ain't gotta make a big performance out of it. Git 'er done.

And then I knew. Then I knew why the man I had inconvenienced, stressed, and cost both time and money, was so very happy. I knew why, after pouring my heart out in Nepal, life was all green lights and walk signs and unexpected upgrades; rainbows, sunsets, and good times. Because all the love you give comes back to you. Not necessarily in the way you expect, or from the people to whom it was given. But sure as day follows night, the love that moves the sun and the other stars sees to it that, in the end, "*The love you take is equal to the love you make.*"

That's how The Beatles put it. For Sir Isaac Newton it was the Third Law of Motion: every action has an equal and opposite reaction. Jewish people call it *ahava*: a feeling of love that comes from the act of giving (*hav*). See how the word itself illustrates the point: that the good feeling (*ahava*) comes from—is created by— the initial act of giving (*ahav*)? Clever, that.

Christians call it reaping and sowing, and in the Sanskrit language of the ancient Indian subcontinent, it's called *karma*: a spiritual principle of cause and effect whereby a person's actions and intentions influence their future. *Karma* is closely linked to the idea of rebirth (*samsara*) in the main religions of the region: Hinduism, Buddhism, Jainism, and Sikhism. Share and be generous with others, *karma* says, and you tee yourself up for a post-death promotion. Keep all your time and energy and ideas and goodwill and money for yourself and, YIKES! Watch out.

No escaping it: what goes around, comes around. It will bite you in the ass, or it will bless you. Possibly in another lifetime, but still—sure as day follows night, folks move up or down the spiritual hierarchy depending on whether they raise others up or bring them down. So don't get distressed about the dictators and demagogues. They'll be destroyed or debased at some point, along with that horrible person in the office and those neighbors from hell. I know, I know. They should by rights be custard-pied in the face or fired next week, but what can I say? Take heart that their *karma* is in the post, and so is yours. All your good deeds will be rewarded in the next lifetime. This is the promise of *karma*. And this is the promise of *mudita* (another Sanskrit word from the Indian subcontinent):

your good deeds will also be rewarded now. Right here, right now, in this lifetime.

Mudita means "vicarious pleasure in another person's happiness." Derived from *modati*, meaning "to rejoice" or "to be happy," *mudita* is the pleasure you get from witnessing another person's joy.

When you encounter a happy person, you feel happy too. The most reliable way to generate that pleasure is, of course, to help another person to become happy. Do something nice for another person—ain't gotta make a big performance out of it; that cheery greeting will do—and the good feeling you generate in them, will generate a good feeling in you.

Mudita is the reason volunteers talk with conviction about how "they gave me more than I ever gave them," and so many billionaires go from making money to giving it away. Literally, they are getting high from giving. That's how the scientific literature describes it: a "helpers' high." A helper's high is a kind of euphoria generated by an altruistic act. It's the same kind of euphoria as is generated by sex, drugs, and rock-n-roll (and chocolate, obviously), because the things we do to help another person activate the same parts of the brain, and stimulate the release of the same neurotransmitters. Yes: being kind activates the same pleasure centers as cocaine and cookies.

Mudita is an ancient spiritual principle proven by modern science. Overwhelmingly proven, in fact. A nationwide study of 2,705 American adults conducted by UnitedHealthcare/ VolunteerMatch in 2017 found that 98 percent of volunteers claim that the act of giving makes *them*, the volunteers, feel happy and joyful. In addition to improved mood, the study found that 79 percent of volunteers reported lower stress levels, and 88 percent reported increased self-esteem by giving back.[8]

I'm going to repeat that in case you were distracted, dumbfounded, or just didn't believe it could possibly be true. After all, a DJ gets to scratch back to that bit of the track that gets everyone dancing; why not me? Here we go—right back around to the hook.

Ninety-eight percent of volunteers claim that the act of giving makes them feel happy. YOU. You you you you you you you. Helping another person feel happy actually makes YOU feel good. The one giving, not only the one getting the support, feels better. One last time: giving to another person makes you feel happy.

I will continue to spin the discs on *mudita*, because it brings even more benefits.

WHAT?

Yes, my dear, yes. It gets better. Ready to know how? Alright, here we go.

Give, and you get a longer life. A meta-analysis of more than fourteen studies—each with an average of 4,928 participants—show that volunteers have 24–47 percent lower mortality rates than non-volunteers.[9]

---

8. "Doing Good is Good for You." UnitedHeath Group. Study on physical, mental and emotional benefits of volunteering, Minnetonka, September 14, 2017. https://www.unitedhealthgroup.com/newsroom/2017/0914studydoinggoodisgoodforyou.html#:~:text=The%20report%2C%20titled%20the%202017,feel%20physically%20healthier%20by%20volunteering.&text=%22At%20UnitedHealthcare%20we%20have%20seen,of%20social%20responsibility%20for%20UnitedHealthcare.

9. "Volunteering by Older Adults and Risk of Mortality: A Meta-Analysis," Okun, Yeung, and Brown. American Psychological Association, *Psychology and Aging*, 2013, Vol. 28, No. 2, 564–577.

Give, and you get greater earnings. Research from the University of Wisconsin–Madison found that younger volunteers go on to enjoy higher earnings and educational achievements.

Give, and you get better mental and physical health. Volunteers of all ages report improved mental health. This includes lower levels of anxiety, depression, and stress. Research by the Harvard School of Public Health, Boston College, University of Michigan and John Hopkins University finds that in addition to feeling better, volunteers' bodies and brains work better too: on average they spend 38 percent less time in hospital, experience less disability, less pain, and enjoy higher levels of well-being. They have lower cholesterol, lower blood pressure, and improved cognitive abilities. Just two to three hours per week confers these many benefits. And people who give money, rather than time, receive health benefits too.[10]

Give, and you get greater satisfaction from spending money. fMRI scans show that when we make charitable donations, the nucleus accumbens—the part of the brain that responds to pleasure—lights up. Ain't gotta make a big performance out of it: the effect happens whether you give the change

---

10. "Chronic Pain Patient to Peer: Benefits and Risks of Volunteering," Arnstein, Vidal, Well-Federman, Morgan, and Caudill, *Pain Management Nurses*, 3(3): 94–103.2002); "Volunteering and Subsequent Health and Well-Being in Older Adults: An Outcome-Wide Longitudinal Approach," Kim, Whillons, Lee, Chen, VanderWeele, *American Journal of Preventive Medicine*, Volume 59, Issue 2, 176–186, August 1, 2020. https://hrs.isr.umich.edu/data-products. "A social model for health promotion for an aging population: initial evidence on the Experience Corps model," Fried, Carlson, Freedman, Glass, Hill, McGill, Rebok, Seeman, Tielsch, Wasik, Zeger, *Journal of Urban Health*, 2004 Mar 1981(1):64–78.

in your pocket or enough to build a hospital wing. That's according to research conducted by the *Harvard Business Review* (and a Texas wrangler).[11] The money we spend on others makes us happier than the money we spend on ourselves. Researchers at the University of British Columbia conducted a statistical analysis on personal spending of people across the United States. They found that regardless of how much income each person made, those who spent more money on others reported greater happiness. Another study that gave students money to either spend on themselves or others found that those who spent the money on others felt happier than those who spent it on themselves.[12]

Nuts, isn't it? Who would have thought?! Not the students participating in the studies. They expected that spending on themselves would make them happier than giving their money away, and were astonished that you git more blessins by giving to others than getting for yourself. Again, ain't gotta make a big performance out of it: the students only had small amounts of money (either a $5 or a $20 bill). So if you want to pay for the entire cast of the Metropolitan Opera for a season, knock yourself out. But if all you've got in your pocket is five bucks and some lint, you can still get a warm glow by giving.

Give, and you get a feeling that you have more time. Surely, this is the big one. Money? You can earn it. Time? No one

---

11. "Feeling Good about Giving: The Benefits (and Costs) of Self-Interested Charitable Behavior," Anik, Aknin, Norton, and Dunn, *Harvard Business Review*, Working Paper 10-012, 2009.
12. Spending Money on Others Promotes Happiness.' Dunn, et al., *Science* Vol. 319, 1687, 21 March 2008, (Washington DC, 2008).

pays that out as a dividend or adds it to their will. Beyond luxury—that Ralph Lauren cape you've had your eye on, the month of Balinese flower baths and dinners at The Ritz—true wealth, surely, is feeling unrushed. That peaceful holiday forgetting what day it is while wandering around in sandals and a sundress, slowly eating ice cream and watching the sun shine on polished marble and glint off golden mosaic. Turns out that giving your time to help another person helps you to access that relaxed feeling. That's according to the findings of experiments run by the business schools of the University of Pennsylvania, Yale, and Harvard.[13] People randomly assigned to do helping tasks (such as writing notes to sick children) on a Saturday morning were more likely to say that their futures felt "infinite." People who helped underprivileged high school students were less likely to agree that time is scarce and more likely to say, "I currently have time to spare." They also went on to both commit to, and actually spend, more time on a paid task. Giving your time away actually makes you feel more time affluent.

I can practically see you: eyes wide, mouth open, mind spinning at this astonishing possibility. How can you expend your limited budget of resources on something, and yet not deplete it? How can you get more satisfaction from helping another person to meet their needs? Surely, since you're in your own body, it would be the other way around? What about the "nice guys finish last" thing? Is the truth that . . . nice guys finish first? Is that why folks like Warren Buffett and Bill Gates and Richard Branson hire entire teams to give

---

13. "Giving Time Gives You Time," Moligner, Chance, and Norton, Psychological *Science*, 2012 Oct 1. 23(10):1233–8.

their money away? What about simple mathematics? Is that not a thing anymore? Have we gone all quantum and weird and wondering, *Does this table really exist? Are we actually here?*

Before we fall down that rabbit hole, let's just assume that yes, the table exists—a fact easily verifiable by walking knees-first into it—and we're really here, and it just so happens that we're wired for kindness. Our physiology is such that we do feel good when we help other people to be happy; and we do become healthier, wealthier, and more satisfied with life when we share what we have with others.

Scientists give a few reasons for this phenomenon; none really get to the root cause of our physiological orientation toward helping. A sense of personal accomplishment; building friendships and getting exercise through volunteer activities; learning new skills; gaining valuable experiences; getting a healthier perspective on our lives by peeking over the fence and realizing the grass under our own feet is quite green actually; feeling a sense of control over social or environmental challenges by doing something about them; gaining status and praise from neighbors and friends. Sanskrit scholars might say: "Well of course we're wired to help others. We're divine creations and so oriented toward love."

But really, who knows? All I can tell you is that this is how it happened: the man I inconvenienced, stressed out, cost money and time, and probably even put in danger, was absolutely delighted. And after I gave my all in Nepal, life was all sunny days and warm nights, streets smelling of roses and *oh! didn't know that was there* money in my pockets. A regular ole hamburger upgraded to a sixteen-ounce steak. BOO YA!

Maybe it's like consciousness and sock-eating washing machines. We just accept that they exist, and that we'll be on this planet for a while, buying an improbable number of socks, and never really knowing why. Why are we here? Where did we come from? Where do the socks go? Why do we get by giving?

Who even cares? Does a DJ need to break it all down and figure out why you're going nuts on the dance floor, hopping up and down, fist pumping? Nope. He's just giving what he's got to give, and getting high on what he's getting back.

And all the while billionaires are giving what they've got, and getting high on what they're getting back. Which is obviously some sort of pleasure that isn't on the menu at any restaurant, available at any five-star hotel, or provided as a members-only benefit at any club. And that pleasure is *mudita*. While we're striving to "make it," the ones who have are all "[shrug] Over it!" apparently, and chasing the pleasure of sharing with others.

There's a clue there, no? If people who can have fleets of Ferraris and wardrobes of Ferragamo are more focused on philanthropy than choosing their next château, maybe we've been asking the wrong questions (What can I get? What do I want? How can I have it?) when the key to getting it all was to ask, "What can I give?"

Which is convenient, because it seems we need to buckle up. A growing global population and diminishing resources means that there's nothing on the horizon but crisis. Social crisis. Political crisis. Economic crisis. Human rights crisis. Crisis of trust in institutions. Crisis in civic space, social cohesion and race relations. Environmental crisis. Biodiversity crisis. Ethical crisis. Pick an adjective, it's probably in crisis.

Here's why you shouldn't be worried: because you are here. You are here—and so am I—and we are made for this.

Literally made for this moment of change and challenge; literally wired to find the happiness, hope, and health you seek by helping others.

And since the global population is increasing, there will be more of us, no? More of us needing the hope that comes from participating in hopeful actions. More of us wanting to get high by raising others up. More of us deciding to part of the making of a better world. More and more of us invited, by the very challenges of this moment, to get what we want, by giving what we have. More and more of us coming alive by connecting to the needs of this moment, and our capacity to address them. More and more of us remembering who we are, and what immense power we have in our hands, and what gifts flow into those hands held out in service.

Sometime I'll tell you what gifts overflowed from mine after I left Nepal.

For now though, I'll say only this: when the preacher said it's like being upgraded from a hamburger to a sixteen-ounce steak, I absolutely knew what he meant. BOO-YA!

———

"I slept and dreamt that life was joy. I awoke and saw that life was service. I acted and behold, service was joy."
—Rabindranath Tagore

9

Blether

Blether (noun, verb)

Pronunciation: blεΘʌr (bleh-thur)

Origin: Scots (Scotland). Derived from *blather* (v.); blither, to talk nonsense, foolish talk. Possibly Scandinavian, Old Norse *blaora,* to mutter, wag the tongue.

Definition: Noun: a chat, story, or informal conversation based on personal stories from daily life. Verb: To chat, have an informal conversation, exchange personal stories in a direct manner: eye-to-eye, mind-to-mind, heart-to heart.

How to use *blether*

Remember my dad, sailor of seas, and teller of tales from all over the blue surface of a spinning globe? My dad was an *Ileach*: a Gaelic word for a person from Islay; a wild and windswept island off the West Coast of Scotland. Islay is in the Highlands of Scotland: a staggeringly beautiful land known for its burns and glens, whiskies and stags, scones and *blethers*.

A burn is a river, a glen is a valley, a whisky is a drink, a stag is a deer, a scone is a baked good, and a *blether* is a chat with folk you meet throughout the day. *Folk* is Highland Scots for people. And since you literally depend on people for survival in a land known for its wild weather, you'd better get to know them. No need to wait for that though: a *blether* is how stranger and acquaintance become friend and family. No need to wait until you've got exciting things to report either: a *blether* is an exchange about whatever is happening in life *the now* (at the moment). It's an informal approach to conversation based on curiosity about whatever is happening in life; not impressive achievements, qualifications, and capabilities. If your hair got stuck in the hairdryer this morning and now looks like something a horse would try to eat, there you go—that's your update. If Roddy from next door accidentally toasted a mouse, you'll be hearing about it. No need to schedule an appointment: most *blethers* are brief, and built into daily activities. If you pop into the local shop for a pint of milk and a box of ammunition, you have a *blether*. If you're waiting at the bus stop, you have a *blether*. If you're driving, you wave or roll down your window for a *wee* (small, short) *blether* to cheer you on your way.

That's what *blethering* is for: to cheer you on your way. Science now shows that chatting even to strangers lifts your mood, and theirs. It gets better: you can use *blethering* to improve your health and longevity, creativity, and performance at work. These evidence-based benefits of a *blether* led Fortune 500 companies to buy conversation training for their managers, and doctors to prescribe social activities for their patients.

Save yourself a kidney stone, why don't you? Just *blether* with folk you come into contact with at the coffee shop and garage, office and supermarket, school and street. This is how you form a community in which you feel at home, and get to where you want to be—whether it's Kho Phi Phi, or food security, or a record deal. Sure, Google maps and permaculture and a book entitled *How To Get A Record Deal* can help. So too can *blethering*: taking the time to talk to people, trusting that what they know is worth saying and that they are worth the time it takes to hear it. I learned that from my dad. Or rather, I learned from him the price we pay when we do not take the time to *blether*.

Once upon a time, merchant seamen sailed all around the world by star and sextant, map and compass. They were the wise men of the sea and lifeblood of the global economy, who could sit with ruler and ream to chart their course from Cape Town to Clydebank, Panama to Plymouth. One day as my father prepared to sail to Sydney, he discovered that those days were over. *BRRRRING BRRRING! BRRING!* "Fax for you, Captain Turner san," said a voice.

The fax contained a remarkable thing: a course from Tokyo to Sydney divined by a supercomputer and printed on giant reams of perforated papers stuck to each other like a giant zigzag, along with an instruction to follow it.

Flipping through the pages, pouring over the dots and lines, my father felt sick. He knew these seas, and how they behaved in storms, and where the winds would be strong, and where—should he follow this plan—he would be when they whipped up a storm. Right there in the storm, with 140 men and 16,000 tons of cargo.

He tried to stop it. He pointed out the dangers to anyone who would listen. He made his case all the way up the hierarchy, until he was told at the top: "New rules, Captain Turner.

New rules. New rules and new tools. You must sail the course that has been given to you. Our insurance is contingent on it, I'm afraid. You have no option, sir. But be assured you're in no danger. Top experts behind this new machine you know; satellites and all sorts. Really excellent stuff. Change with the times and all that. Good day [click]."

Maybe they're right, my dad thought slowly. *Maybe they're right. Maybe the machine knows best. Maybe it'll all be plain sailing.* So he donned his uniform—cap under arm—and set out to the port, to join his ship and set sail for Sydney—through, as it happens, the deepest water in the world.

The Challenger Deep in the Mariana trench is the deepest known point on the planet. If Mount Everest were placed here, it would be covered by more than a mile of water. Yup, the depth of the Challenger Deep is 10,994 meters below sea level. That's 35,814 feet, 11 kilometers. Seven miles of water. It is, quite literally, the worst place on the planet to be stuck in a storm. And my father was. His ship was like a piece of Lego tossed on the vast swell of its violent waters. As he saw the wall of water towering above the boat, he thought, *This is it.*

There's a break in every wind—did you know that? It's some of the sea-faring trivia I picked up over the years. Using the microseconds of grace afforded by that break in the winds, and an uncharacteristic yelling phone call down to the Engine Room, my father got out of that storm. He sailed his own course to Sydney Harbor.

I remembered that story only recently. It came to mind vividly, from nowhere, more than thirty years after I heard it in a somnolent state. And there it remained for days, turning in my head as I wondered why. Why? Why am I remembering this now?

Perhaps it's a warning. A warning of the (practical, personal) dangers of not taking the time to talk to people, trusting that what they have to say is worth hearing, and that they are worth the time and attention to really hear it. Sure, artificial intelligence and satellites and science have their place. But so too do people. So too does what they know from their own lives, and which they can share with those who take the time to hear it.

Perhaps it's a reminder. A reminder that we are the latest in a long line of folk who came through hell and high water, fire and flood, typhoon and tempest, screaming storm and swollen sea for fifty thousand years, using the knowledge they shared with the tongue in their heads and the ears on its side.

Perhaps it's a message of hope. A message of hope that we can do it again. We can use the very same tools that made us who we are to become who we can be: the ones who create the future. The ones who use the most powerful knowledge of all to create the best of all possible worlds. What's the most powerful knowledge of all? The knowledge that you matter. You matter. I matter. We all matter. Everyone matters. Matters enough for you to take the time to hear what they have to say: eye-to-eye, mind-to-mind, heart-to-heart.

How I discovered *blether*

The thing about Scotland is that so much of it is so beautiful, you can lose yourself in it. Lose yourself in the mountains and trees, lochs and skies. Lose a sense of yourself, and time. You can ride and walk and run for hours—partly because it may take that long to reach the nearest shop or pub or tea room. And partly because, once you get going, there really doesn't seem to be any reason to stop. All the petty concerns of life—timetables to observe; emails to be sent or replied to; meetings to be organized; plans to be made or executed—don't exist. The land invites you to step outside yourself, and quite unconsciously you do. Into what I believe is called "the eternal bliss."

Lovely.

Until midges start to bite, the darkness closes in, and you realize you are lost. Actually lost. Not in the "eternal bliss" or "the infinite now" or "all that is." Just lost. In rural Scotland. In the dark. Far from your lodgings, with dodgy bike lights.

The only obvious thing to do is this: knock on the door. A door. Any door. And where I'm from, at least, this is what will happen: someone with a smiley face in a cozy sweater will say, "Och! Come in! Sit here *a graigh* (my dear)." You will be pointed to a comfy fabric sofa. And there you will sit, absorbed slightly by softened cushions while a small dog sniffs your feet, looks into your eyes, trots about with tail wagging—*a guest! a guest!*—before settling down in front of the fire, snuffling. Tea will be served, and the contents of a biscuit barrel revealed.

Yes, that's how we like our treats in Scotland: by the barrel. You will be encouraged to take both the Trio and the Twix between which your hand wavers; and while you lift your cup for a swig of a soothing sweet, softly steaming brew, a little stack of jaffa cakes will be plonked on your plate.

As you munch, the dog snuffles and chews the corner of a carpet off-cut by the hearth. As you sip, your host jaggles a poker in the grate and brushes bits of log onto a knee-length skirt. As the fire crackles and the faint smell of smoke—earthy, grounding—enfolds you, a feeling of soporific bliss settles in. The scene is set. We are ready for a *blether*.

"Where d'ya stay *a graigh*?" asks your host (let's call her Flossie), in a sing-songy voice. To your response she says, "Ooh! America, is it?!"

"Austria, eh?! I've heard it's jees lovely there!"

"New Zealand, are ya really? Ye've come along way then, eh?"

"And are ye having a good time?"

"And how long are you visiting?"

"And did you get over on the ferry okay?"

"You were lucky, *a graigh*," says a gentleman in a large armchair facing the TV, as he raises a cheese scone to his mouth. "You jees never know with MacBrayne's these days. Somebody in Port Askaig could turn a hairdryer on, and they'll cancel the sailing, eh? They'll hufftae get a new boat or summat, so folk can get aboot."

He turns back to face the TV, shaking his head.

Flossie glances briefly at the goggle box to see what is entrancing her husband, tells you that they'll give you a lift home "in a *wee whiley* (short time), once you've warmed up," then enquires about the places you've been and the things that you've seen on your trip. She tells you about people from your country once known to relatives and locals, and the time their son went on holiday there with his girlfriend not so long ago. Or was it a neighboring country? Yes now I come to think of it, it was a totally different place. "But anyway! Won't you have another cup of tea, *a graigh*?"

Before you answer, Flossie rises, teapot in hand, wincing slightly from a pinched nerve in a bended knee, and walks, a bit unevenly, to the kitchen. From behind a cupboard, over the sound of a boiling kettle, she calls out, "And some more jaffa cakes?"

Before you respond, our man in the armchair says with glorious *teuchter* (Highland) gusto: "AYE! BRING THAT BOX O' JAFFA CAKES OUT HERE, HEN! SHE LIKES THE JAFFA CAKES!"

He turns to you and says, "You'll no have had yer *tea* (dinner), will ye, *a graigh*?!"

Before you have a chance to reply: "AND A SANDWICH, HEN! SHE'S NO HAD HER TEA!"

Already quite full, but enjoying the savory tastes of ham and cheese, your pal in the armchair looks at you approvingly: "Right, y'are, *a graigh*, you've got tae take care o'yerself."

As you flex your pink-socked feet in the soothing warmth of the roaring fire, you learn about things you might enjoy while you're here: the Duck Race next weekend; the fête on Saturday. "There's a greasy pole and there's bands and a three-legged race and an egg-and-spoon competition, and all sorts for young folk like yourself," your host explains.

"And there's bands!" the gentleman says, sipping his brew. "Very good bands, so they are,"

Flossie continues. "*Oor* pipe band came third in the Championships in Paisley, so they did. The drummers are fantastic!"

"*Aye*, the drummers are good," the gentleman chips in, still staring at the screen.

You show photos of the huge red Highland cows you saw by the lighthouse, and hear about Angus McNab who keeps them. He is a farmer. Also a lighthouse keeper, policeman, captain of the local football team, manager of the local campsite, member of the pipe band, supplier of water and barley to the local distillery, and also wins the tossing of the sheaf competition at The Show every year "Even though he's getting on for seventy-odd years, would you look at that? And it's a wee shame you won't be here for The Show yourself because it's great for young folk."

"*Aye!* It's a right old *hoorealey!*" says our man in the armchair, with a chortle.

"What's a *hoorealey?*" you ask.

"A right old yee-ha, *a graigh.* A right old yee-ha."

Blue eyes sparkling, Flossie bites her lip and smiles: "*Aye.* It gets a bit wild in the night time, so they say. But they're farmers, *a graigh;* what d'ya expect?"

There's a faint sound of rustling leaves and swaying branches. A gust of wind billows in the chimney. A carriage clock ticks on the mantle; its sound slow and deliberate and not mattering at all because this is tea time, and we're having a *blether.*

You can *blether* anywhere, and with anyone: the person serving you in a shop, giving you your post, passing you on the street, standing next to you at the bus stop, or behind you at the coffee shop. Just a few seconds or minutes while you go about your business; no need to schedule an appointment. Longer exchanges do happen of course—a friend over for tea, drinks out with colleagues, a meal with your mum—but these are the outliers. Most are brief *wee* exchanges with strangers and folk you barely know. All are characterized by curiosity about what's happening in life at this moment (*the now*): mundane details or extraordinary occurrences, blended with a bit of humor and encouragement.

Forget reeling off the contents of this week's *Economist* or what you learned from your podcast on the rise and fall of the Persian Empire—a *blether* is a simpler thing. An easy exchange about the details of daily life, a humble human connection through words spoken "eye to eye, mind to mind, heart to heart." Sometimes translated as a story, to *blether* is to share happenings from life, your real life. It doesn't matter that you're not the Queen of Britain, Northern Ireland and Other Territories, Head of the Commonwealth and Defender of the Faith. It matters that you exist. It matters only that you are here. And so am I. Standing by the same kettle, or in the queue for the same toilet, or living upstairs, or working next door, or choosing among the same range of sandwiches. And we are here together. That is why we *blether*.

Chit chat? Idle chatter? Prattle? Small talk? Time wasting? Jibber jabber? Distraction?

As you like it.

A *blether* is a proven way to brighten your day, improve your health, and build the community that makes life better. It creates the empathy that makes people you wouldn't necessarily choose to have a cup of tea with a bit more lovable. And all the while, it gives you the fresh perspectives and information that people with a different vantage point can provide, and the new ideas that move all of humanity forward. All that and a cup of tea, if you're lucky.

So, "How would you feel about striking up conversation on your morning commute?" That is the question that researchers at the University of Chicago asked bus and train commuters, as they set up experiments to explore the impact of *blethering* on happiness, energy level, and productivity.

And how about you? How would you feel about having a *wee blether* on your morning commute? Or with the barista, shopkeeper, sales assistant, neighbor? How do you think it would impact your happiness, energy, and productivity?

"*Errr* . . . not sure I'd like that very much. I'd be embarrassed to try; worried about bothering people. Plus it could be exhausting to listen to people go on about things that have nothing to do with me. I'd rather use that time to do something productive. Gosh it could even be dangerous—plenty of nutcases around you know. Nope. Not gonna do it. Just to confirm: it's a no."

"Do you think other people would want to talk to you?"

"No. No . . . I reckon most people would think I was nuts or trying to recruit them to some sort of spiritual group or something. Or get some money from them."

"Would anyone want to speak, do you think?"

"Well, I suppose some would. Less than half though, I'd say. Most people would just want to be left alone to prepare for the day, I imagine. Do their work, read the news, go on Facebook or something."

You're in good company. That's how the study started. The research leads asked local bus and train commuters how they would feel about striking up a conversation on their morning commute—compared to either sitting on their own quietly focusing on the day ahead, or doing whatever they normally do, like reading, listening to music, looking at social media, emailing, etc. The majority predicted that *blethering* (connection condition) would be the worst option—much better to keep themselves to themselves and quietly focus their thoughts (solitude condition), or do whatever they normally do (control condition).

They were wrong.

Study participants randomly assigned to have a *blether* had the most pleasant commute. Not only did the chatty commuters report having the highest mood and most pleasant journey, they had a significantly more positive experience than those sitting alone. They had no less energy at the end of the commute, and no significant difference in their level of productivity.

The findings were the same for introverts and extroverts: both were happier when they talked to a stranger, no matter how extroverted they perceived themselves to be. The only difference is expectation: introverts were more likely to under-estimate the positive consequences of a *blether*. And yet, they too felt happier when they tried it.

Nine times. The researchers ran nine experiments to check and double check that their surprising findings could actually be true. Alas, separate experiments in buses and taxis yielded similar results: participants expected that chatting to strangers would be unpleasant and unproductive, and that being alone would be much better. And again and again—and again and again and again—their experience was the exact opposite of what they expected. The people who took the time to *blether* had the best time.

A separate experiment in a waiting room found that the people who struck up conversation, and the person that they talked to, both enjoyed the chat. Not one participant had trouble finding someone to talk to, and a number even had conversations so interesting and enjoyable that they planned to meet again soon.

So you see, lovely one? The good news is that the bad news is wrong. People are usually happy to chat for a few minutes, friendly, not in the least bit threatening, and able to elicit a feeling of happiness that you cannot access alone, or from your book or phone or i-thing.

By all means organize a holiday to Hawaii, set the credit card on fire at Hotel Chocolat, sip your adaptogenic brew, do your breathing, aromatherapy, acupuncture, gratitude journal, grounding, forest bathing, and those yoga moves you found on the back of a box of tea. Also, ask a stranger about themselves, and say a little about you. A simple way to wellness, word by word.

You are wired to feel well with a *blether*. Research at the University of Wisconsin-Madison shows that chatting reduces levels of salivary cortisol (a biomarker of stress), and increases levels of urinary oxytocin (a hormone involved in the formation and maintenance of positive relationships, and used to treat depression and anxiety). In other words, a wee *blether* actually alters your biology in ways that make you feel good. Feel good, and do well. Because *blethering* isn't only pleasant; it's practically useful too. Think about it. Have you ever had a random chance encounter that brought surprising benefits from the blue: interesting information from a relative that really got you thinking, an idea that occurred to you in conversation with an acquaintance, a staggeringly useful suggestion from a stranger?

Business executive Judith Glaser noticed that strange phenomenon too. She saw that in some organizations, brilliant ideas bubbled from staff interactions like a foam party—boosting these firms to the top of the Fortune 500— while others crashed and burned with a market offering that excited no one. So Judith worked with teams at management consulting firm the CreatingWe Institute and software company Qualtrics to measure how different types of conversational behaviors influence the chemistry and functioning of the brain to empower creativity and productivity.

Their findings, reported in the *Harvard Business Review*, found that the ways of communicating considered efficient, professional, and business-as-usual in the workplace—information transactions of basic facts, stripped down stats and brief updates—create changes in brain chemistry that close down the very part of the brain that enables stellar performance. It's called the prefrontal cortex, and it's the bit of the brain responsible for executive functioning: the part that enables you to develop ideas, plans, and the will to follow through on them. The capacity for concentration, focus, impulse control, working memory, abstract thinking, reasoning, organization, and creativity are also seated here. In conclusion, you're basically a genius: the machinery of miracles, from the internet and the umbrella to *The Great Gatsby* and *Blood on the Tracks*, is right there behind your forehead.

Trouble is, you can't always access it. Anytime you feel like you have to prove something, say something interesting, convince someone of anything, or that people are judging you, not really listening, or not understanding what you say, you lose access to this brilliant part of you. These types of conversational behaviors activate the amygdala—the so-called *primitive* part of the brain—putting you in a defensive, protective freeze/fight/flight mode. With the primitive brain running the show, you're basically mining the junkyard of the mind and hoping to find treasure. Ever wondered why meetings seem like such a fruitless waste of time, even with smart people at the table? Ever wondered what killed your creativity and all that sparkle and brilliance you just know is in there somewhere? Wonder no more. Mystery solved. It was the amygdala. In the meeting room. With the PowerPoint.

The good news is that a *blether* makes it better. The conversational behaviors of a *blether*—honesty about what's on your mind, curiosity about what's happening in another person's life, based on concern about them in general, rather than on what they have achieved—generates oxytocin, puts the body and brain into a relaxed state, and opens up its creative potential. BINGO! Individuals and teams with this kind of conversational style perform better. So much better that coaching and certification programs are available based on this research, aiming to help professionals learn to converse in a way that drives innovation and a positive, productive organizational culture. I reckon they could just go to the Highlands of Scotland—why not? Make a holiday out of it. Do your training over a beer in a bar while fiddlers play by a fire.

From the Highlands of Scotland with love: another word, another way to feel good, do well, and live longer. The word is *blether*, and you are welcome.

Wait a minute. Live longer? Live longer?! What's this now?

Aye, a graigh (yes, my love). Live longer. As long as you don't eat too many scones, I suppose, a *wee blether* will keep you in fine fettle.

Cigarettes. Cakes. Cookies. Candy. Crack. Cocaine. Everyone knows these things are unhealthy. But what about loneliness? Apparently, it's more common than you might imagine, and getting worse: a nationwide survey of 20,000 Americans conducted by the University of California, Los Angeles, in 2018, found that 54 percent of respondents consider themselves to be lonely.[14] Fast forward two years, and three in five adults, a whopping 61 percent of the population, are lonely.[15] Since loneliness is actually deadly (more on that in a minute), the British government appointed a minister to deal with the issue. Dr. Helen Stokes-Lampard, chair of the British Royal College of General Practitioners, is leading a change in the practice of medicine to include a concern for patients' social health. And Dr. Vivek Murty, the nineteenth surgeon general of the United States, is on a mission to include what he terms "the healing power of human connection" in medicine.

It makes sense when you see the statistics: social isolation is as dangerous as smoking fifteen cigarettes a day. An initial Brigham Young University global meta-study of data from 148 studies involving 300,000 participants showed that people with strong social relationships are 50 percent less likely to die prematurely than those with weak social ties. The impact of social isolation on lifespan is greater than obesity, alcoholism, or inactivity. People who are lonely are more likely to develop coronary heart disease and stroke, cognitive decline and dementia, high blood pressure, depression, and anxiety. They are more likely to have lower-quality sleep, immune system dysfunction, impulsive behavior, and impaired judgment. Deprivation of social contact activates the same systems as physical violence, meaning that we are literally physiologically harmed by a lack of human interaction.

---

14. Cigna. (2018). Cigna U.S. Loneliness Index: Survey of 20,000 Americans examining behaviors driving loneliness in the United States. https://www.cigna.com/assets/docs/newsroom/loneliness-survey-2018-updated-fact-sheet.pdf
15. Cigna (2020). U.S. Loneliness Index. https://www.cigna.com/about-us/newsroom/studies-and-reports/combatting-loneliness/

Hot diggity damn. Who'd have thought?!

The good news is that this little skull-and-crossbones section of our story ends well, with the happy knowing that it's easy to avoid becoming one of all the lonely people. Just use the portable social equipment stored about your skull. *Blethering* leads to measurable improvements in health indicators from hypertension and hyperglycemia to depression and life expectancy. That's why social prescribing, which connects patients to community-based activities where they can have a *wee blether*, is now a medical protocol championed by leading physicians—and by vast swathes of the Scottish population. Perhaps, by the end of these pages, you'll join us in the B-Team. We may not be as professional or efficient as the A-Team, but we're happier, healthier, and—to everyone's surprise—we perform better too.

The other bit of good news (bear with me now) is that *blethering* can change the world.

I know, I know. I never would have believed it myself. Except, I lived it.

I was seventeen years old, sitting on the sofa down the road at number six: a white house on a small hill with green fields to the back and the sea to the front. On a clear day, you can see Ireland through the window. On that particular evening, the sky was a shade of red and purple so mesmerizing that I didn't care to look at what's on the horizon, only the improbable wash of colors high above it. I had left school and worked as a waitress, sales assistant, babysitter, glass and ashtray collector, and finally saved up enough pennies to go on a solo trip through America, Australasia, and Asia. Soon I would be off.

Ooh! That's exciting! Are you excited?

Yes. Also: terrified.

Why?

Well . . . *ssshhhh* now; keep this to yourself. I'm . . . *uh* . . . slightly navigationally challenged.

What? But didn't you say your father was a sailor?

Yes, yes. My father was a sailor. My grandfather was a sailor. My great-grandfather was a sailor. Cousins, uncles, all sailors. Proper sailors. Sailors who could reel off all thirty-six points of the compass in a split second, chart a course all over our blue and lovely planet with rulers and maps and sextants and compasses, and the light of the silvery moon, and a sea of stars above a sea of water with a whole aquatic world under its surface. Sailors who knew a Pacific sky from an Atlantic sky, and how to tie twenty kinds of knots and calculate nautical miles and fathoms and leagues and read a barometer.

Me? I feel sorry for anyone who asks me for directions. No one in my family wants me anywhere near a map. And should a sailor ever offer me the wheel, I know that the best option for everyone is a polite but firm, "No, thank you." Trust me.

And yet. There I was. At a time before iPhones and Uber and WhatsApp and GoogleMaps, worried and wondering, *How am I going to do this? How am I even going to get to those hostels with the hairy soaps and find those urban internet cafes with the dial-up connections and keyboards worn away to clear plastic, let alone the millions of miles between them?*

For some reason—although I am now realizing it's likely because my brain was massaged with oxytocin while *blethering* over tea and a Kit-Kat—I forgot my embarrassment and mentioned my concern. I'm not sure how I danced around the apple tree to explain it, but I'll never forget the response.

First of all, you should know that Stan Richards moved from Newcastle to the Highlands of Scotland about forty years ago, but sounds like he might have arrived on this afternoon's ferry in a toon army T-shirt. He's a jeans-and-boots wearing, straight-talking man's man. He can mend a car, build a house, smell a rat, and put anyone in their place. Today was my day. When I mentioned my "slight problem," he turned from the TV and looked—nay, stared—right at me, fixing his bright-blue eyes on me so forcefully that I froze in my seat. Then he said these words, "What are you worried about, man? You've got a tongue in yer heid, have you not?"

Blue eyes blazing, voice accusing, brow furrowed to a deep crease between peepers staring at me so pointedly that they seem to be poking me for an answer, Stan's words were wands, exorcising all doubt.

Yes. Yes. Yes I do have a tongue in ma heid. And for that matter, two ears on its side.

A tongue in ma heid, two ears on its side. Neuro-audial technology neatly stored on my skull: a convenient substitute for all the things I did not know, and all the things I cannot do. Technology that made it possible for my ancestors—heck, all of our ancestors—to come through hell and highwater, fire and flood, plague and poverty, conflict and every kind of crisis from economic to atomic. Technology that created our very species and entire civilization. Could this same technology help me get to the airport? Yeah . . . it might help a bit.

So off I went. And with the tongue in my head and the ears on its side, there was no destination I couldn't find. No way I couldn't find, nothing I couldn't do, and nothing I couldn't help others to do, in a twenty-year adventure that started in America, Australasia, and Asia, and continued through Europe, Africa, the Middle East and Pacific.

Take Indonesia for example. There I was, waiting at an airport on one of its 17,000 islands with my red-and-brown leather tote under my arm when suddenly, a petite lady in a navy-blue skirt suit started waving her arms about and yelling, "No fligh! No fligh! Fligh cancel!"

After enquiries, I discovered that due to some sort of bureaucratic bungle, the airline had lost its license and the flight was cancelled... forever. Not going to leave today. Not going to leave tomorrow. Not going to leave... ever. Which seemed like a bummer because it was the only airline running the route. Alas, a fellow traveler I'd been *blethering* with wasn't worried. He said so: "No worries! You'll be able to get there from Darwin, I reckon. Come to stay with us in Darwin! Overnight at our house, get a good night's sleep, proper bed, nice Lush products in the shower—wife loves 'em—then fly out the next day."

I was, indeed, at my duty station the next day, well rested and smelling of patchouli.

It's good to know, isn't it? Good to know that even if you are phoneless and friendless in a foreign land, you can use the tongue in yer heid and the ears on its side, and be just fine. Good to know that there's nowhere on earth you will go, and nothing you will ever try to do, that people can't advise you on or help you with. Good to know that you have the most powerful creative force in history attached to your head. And when you have a problem, it might help a bit.

Consider Nepal. After spending tens of millions of dollars to improve justice and security, impunity rates were unchanged. Crime was proliferating, and many Nepalis still didn't feel safe even years after the worst of the war was over. After countless studies to find the source of the problem and projects to fix it—each with their own budget and team—the problem remained: less than 2 percent of criminals were actually held accountable. Time for a *blether*.

Police: "Has the number of court judgments increased? Didn't know that."

Court: "Really? But it's your job to act on them."

Police: "Well yes, but we never receive any."

Court: "Don't you?"

Police: "No."

Court: "Really?"

Police: "No."

Court: "Oh. How about we bring you the list then; say every Friday?"

Police: "Okay."

Within four months: *duh-duh-duh-daaaa*! A 177 percent increase in judgments executed. And all for the price of some tea and biscuits. Which is good to know, isn't it? Good to know that if *blethering* can't "change the world" exactly, it can certainly fix a few of the things that had kept it from being a bit better.

"Change the world."

"Create a better world."

"Be the change."

"Put a dent in the universe."

Maybe it's because they've been heavily featured in ad campaigns for companies claiming a social consciousness, or because I've been at the UN for the last thirteen years, or because I went through a stage of watching those motivation videos on YouTube with someone huffing and puffing while they lift weights, as though a few more bicep curls will end global poverty or "Save Africa" (whatever that means). Whatever the reason, these words can seem a little stale sometimes, no?

And yet, we're drawn to them. Drawn to change the world in some way, through an award-winning endeavor or the kind of career that ends with a biopic and a bronze statue in Central Park. Or kids who get on that plinth in the Park. Or an eightieth birthday party where folk praise you for being such a champ.

We're drawn to it even when figuring out how to pay the rent and buy Christmas presents with the change you find down the back of the sofa is the challenge of the moment, and you feel about as far from a write-up in *The Times* as Texas is from Tonga. But what to do? Might as well accept reality, as it is. Starry-eyed kids, creatine-munching muscle men, you and me: all quietly drawn to put a dent in the universe. All inspired by the glorious possibility of leaving this world a little better than it is now, for just a few people. A little closer to how they themselves would like it to be.

The good news is that you can. The even better news is that it isn't that hard. Law reform and strategy reviews and policy adjustments and plans and projects and programs and politicians and prophets and professors and PhDs and professionals and CEOs in every sphere and sector have their place. Of course they do. But so do you and I. So does all that we can do with our minds and our hearts, our hands and our feet. So too does what we know through what we have lived. And so too, most definitely, does the change we can affect with the tongue in our heads and the ears on its side.

I know it's true because I saw it in many places, and came to understand it in one: San Quentin Prison, California.

It's not the Seychelles, I'll give you that. And this unexpected information about what I'd be doing over the next few months seemed to have caused my elderly Assyrian landlady to short-circuit. From under crepe-paper eyelids, her cloudy eyes flickered back and forth, and her head bobbed jauntily from side to side. "What's a nice girl like you doing in a place like that?" Mrs. Davoodian asked finally, over glasses as thick as the bottom of jam jars.

Petite and polite, well-spoken and well-dressed, I'm not your average jail bird.

Long story short: I wanted to find out how change happens. How does positive, life-enhancing change really happen? Helping to create a more peaceful world is a wonderful thing— of course it is. Angels start singing, doves flutter across the sky, adults shed tears of joy, and children cheer at the mere thought of it. Helping nations go from war and poverty to peace and progress is also brilliant. Flags wave, crowds cheer, and there are parties in the street—like that time in Lebanon when the world watched and wondered, "Are they dancing or protesting?"

It's all fantastic angel, dove, and DJ-worthy stuff. But do we know how to do it? Do we really? Walk before you can run, and all that: do we know how to change just one life for the better? Do we know how to help one person go from a life of violence, to peacefully contributing to a healthy society? Apparently not. Recidivism (reoffending) rates are 20–63 percent even in wealthy countries—and close to 90 percent in many of those affected by conflict. So imagine my delight to discover a project that was doing the "impossible" thing:

helping lifers change so completely that they could convince the parole board of their eligibility for release, and live successful, good lives on the outside.

Eager to find out how they were achieving such staggering results, I volunteered to help. And this is what I discovered. The project was teaching valuable skills. Communication skills, in fact. You need them to form good relationships, get a job, manage stressful situations without punching someone in the face and such, right? But other volunteer-run projects were teaching valuable things too, like literacy, numeracy, arts, technical career skills, cognitive behavioral therapy, yoga. What made this one special?

Truth be told, we could have taught basket weaving. What made the difference was that we listened. Communication involves speaking and listening, and we listened. We listened as folk *blethered* about whatever is happening in life in *the now*—breakfast this morning, break time yesterday, remembered incidences from the distant past, desires for the future, funny moments, or interesting reflections—just, you know, whatever. And do you know? For many of the guys, this was the first time that anyone had really listened to them. The first time in their life that anyone let them know that what they have to say is important. The first time they had a sense that they are worthy of the most valuable thing another person has: their time and attention.

Worthy of the time and attention even of strangers: unpaid people who spend their own petrol money and give minutes of their own time to *blether*. Worthy just because you're here. Worthy whatever you have to say. Worthy because what you say is important—important to me, important in general. You don't have to report big achievements or exciting events or progress and plans. You won't get a biscuit for saying particular things, or for scoring points on a scale, or performing a role. There is no scale. There are no points. There is no role to perform. And you'll get a biscuit anyway: either an actual baked item, or the sweet, soothing affirmation that you are worthy of another person's time and attention, no matter what.

And if your entire life experience to this point has pretty much amounted to a case for why you are worth nothing more than some bad food and a few minutes of movement behind thick brick walls with bars, that might really mean something. If all you have known is difficulty and discrimination, suffering and struggle, surrounded by people who say and circumstances that suggest that you are worthless, a *blether* might just negate that narrative. And a new narrative might just be the starting point for a new life. A new life based on the knowledge that you matter. To *blether* is to act from that knowledge, and to affirm it.

Which is why I know that you can change the world, my love. With work that wins Grammy Awards and Oscars and Nobels and Pulitzer Prizes and Instagram followers and *Vogue* spreads and your name in big letters on big buildings and this: taking the time to *blether*. Taking the time to talk to the people around you eye-to-eye, mind-to-mind, heart-to-heart. Giving another person the most valuable thing you have—your time and attention—knowing that in addition to lifting your own spirits, you call forth the potential of theirs. The potential to do, create, be, have, endure, overcome, traverse, and transform all things.

Yes, all things. All things. After all, no one thought that parliamentarians of cities that profited from the Atlantic slave trade would vote to end it in 1807. No one thought that Zulus fighting with spears and shields would beat the bayonets and bullets of the most powerful army on earth in 1879. No one thought that Black South Africans would win the vote in 1994.

But here we are. Here we are. Here we are in a world changed by people who came to believe that they could become the bigger, freer version of themselves, and that there was a force within them that could overcome the obstacles in their way.

That force within is the human spirit.

And the hidden power of language is the ability to call it forth, word by word.

———

"Well of course you've got to talk to people! You know; show an interest." —Heather Turner

Epilogue

I felt called to write this book of words for a better world, and I said, "Yes!"

Now I invite you to say yes to what's next: the world's first multilingual dictionary for global citizenship. A digital platform to inspire action for the Sustainable Development Goals (SDGs), by sharing proven practices, principles, and perspectives through single words that help those good ideas travel far, and stick fast, in hearts and minds globally.

What words matter to you? What words have changed your life, or helped to make it more enjoyable? What words could help another person to understand how you see, appreciate how you think, and learn from how you live? What are your words to live by?

Words of wisdom, wellness, and wonder: within you are a wealth of words and stories that can enrich our world. It's true for every human; it's true for you. Language shaped who we all are, and will continue to shape who we become.

Why not use words that help us feel good and do well? Words that make us come alive to the possibilities around us; feel inspired by the prospect of a brighter future, become proactive in creating it, and energized by doing so. After all, the positive energy that goes into positive things flows through you first. And this is what I want for you: for you to enjoy the good feeling that comes from doing good things, and the hope that comes from hopeful actions.

If you want the same, please contact me at www.lucy turner.org, or on social media. Together, we can turn this book of my stories, written for you, into a digital collection of our words and stories, for all who may be served by them.

Taking *9 Wonder Words* from a book to a digital project together will be a way for us to protect the knowledge held in endangered languages; promote intercultural understanding; share proven solutions to practical problems and the perspectives that make life good and enjoyable, no matter what. This can be a way for us to do more to celebrate the life-enhancing wisdom in all our cultures, and for me to continue to be part of your life and learn from your wisdom and words.

I'd love to travel further with you, because *tu'ulun*. I need you, and we all need each other.

Glossary

Aamukaste (Finnish noun): Dew sparkling like jewels on branches and blades of grass.

Abracadabra, هَلُّلِ دُمْحَلْأَهِ (Hebrew exclamation, believed to derive from Aramaic ארבדכ ארבא): Incantation meaning "I create as I speak; it will be created by my words."

Ahava, הבהא (Hebrew noun): Love.

Alakazam (Arabic exclamation, believed to derive from Arabic مسَقَلا) Incantation used to invoke magical power or indicate an instantaneous transformation or appearance.

Alhamdulillah (Arabic exclamation): "Praise be to God" or "Thanks to God." Expression of gratitude uttered even in undesirable situations, in anticipation of a benefit to derive from those situations.

Arepa (Spanish noun): Corn griddle cake made from pre-cooked cornmeal, popular in Colombia and Venezuela.

Aye (Scots adverb): Yes.

Babushka (Russian noun): Grandmother, or elderly woman.

Bandha, बंद (Nepali noun): Strike or protest; shutdown.

Bideshi, वदिशी (Nepali noun): Foreigner.

Blether (Scots noun, verb): Informal conversation based on exchanging personal stories; to have a chat involving personal stories from daily life.

Ble, μπλε (Modern Greek adjective): Blue.

Brahmin, ब्राह्मण (Sanskrit noun): Member of the priestly (highest) class in the Hindu caste system.

Cachapa (Spanish noun): Pancake made from corn.

Chiya, चिया (Nepali noun): Milky, spiced tea.

Dalit, दलित (Sanskrit noun): Member of the so-called ‹untouchable› (lowest) class in the Hindu caste system.

Dhoti, धोती (Sanskrit noun): Garment resembling baggy, knee-length trousers.

Dorje, རྡོ་རྗེ་ (Tibetan noun): Tibetan Buddhist symbol and ritual object.

Drala, དགྲ་བླ་ (Tibetan noun): Invisible, non-physical energy believed to inhabit the air element, and which can protect humans, and link them to a divine power and beauty.

Entelechy, ἐντελής (Greek noun): Full realisation of potential; linked to Aristotelian concept that each object possesses an inherent potential.

Favela (derived from Portuguese, noun): Shanty town or 'slum.'

Fisselig (German adjective): Flustered to the point of incompetence; intense feeling of overwhelm usually brought about by intense and incessant requests.

Ghalazio, γαλάζιο (Modern Greek adjective): Azure, light blue.

Gökotta (Swedish noun): Literally translated as 'early cuckoo,' this word refers to a tradition practiced since the early 1900s, wherein Swedish families get up early on Ascension Day to hear cuckoo birds sing—usually with a packed breakfast to enjoy as they look for the birds and hear their song.

Gozar (Spanish verb): To enjoy; to take pleasure; to feel good; to be carefree.

Gozo (Spanish noun): Joy; enjoyment; pleasure; satisfaction.

Guising (Scots noun): Customary practice whereby young people dressed in costume go from house-to-house at Halloween, reciting verses, performing skits, telling jokes, or singing songs in exchange for food. Believed to be the origin of the American tradition of 'trick-or-treating.'

Hav, בה (Hebrew verb): Root of verb 'to love;' also means 'to give.'

Hola (Spanish salutation): Hello.

Homo sapiens (Latin noun): Human; literally 'wise man.'

Hòro-gheallaidh, 'hoorealey' (Scottish Gaelic noun): A large, lively party; informal, energetic celebration.

Jajajaja (Spanish exclamation): Expression of amusement. Equivalent to 'hahahaha' in English.

Jeelie piece (Scots noun): Jam sandwich; piece of bread and jam.

Jindagi yestai ho, जीवन त्यस्तै हो (Nepali phrase): Life's like that; such is life.

Karma, कर्म (derived from Sanskrit noun): A force produced by a person's actions, which influences them positively or negatively.

Kay garnay? के गर्ने (Nepali phrase): What to do?

Khoire, कुइरे (Nepali adjective): White-skinned; slang word typically used to refer to a light-skinned foreign person in Nepal.

Komorebi, 木漏れ日 (Japanese noun): Sunlight filtering through trees.

Kouman ou ye? (Haitian Creole phrase): How are you?

Khukri, खुकुरी (Nepali noun): A type of knife traditionally associated with the highly respected and admired Nepali-speaking Gurkhas of Nepal.

Linguicide (English noun): Death of a language; language extinction.

Matrika, मातृका (Sanskrit noun): Meaning 'mother' or 'divine mother', this word is also used to refer to the Hindu goddess of the alphabet and letters.

Matrika Shakti, मातृकाशक्ति (Sanskrit noun): The creative energy in the letters that make up words; a subtle strength behind words; the creative power of the sound energy in letters.

Modati, मोदति (Pali verb): To rejoice; to enjoy oneself; to be happy.

Mudita, मुदिता (Sanskrit noun): Vicarious pleasure in another person's happiness. Sympathetic or unselfish joy in the good fortune of others. A celebration of the happiness and achievement of others.

Naya Nepal, नयाँ नेपाल (Nepali noun): New Nepal.

Pabellón (Spanish noun): Traditional Venezuelan dish composed of shredded beef, rice and black beans that had been stewed.

Paisa, पैसा (Nepali noun): A unit of money equivalent to one hundredth of a rupee; money.

Parole (French noun): Word; music; lyrics. Common usage: *avoir la parole* (to have the floor); *donner la parole à quelqun* (give the floor to someone; to 'hand over'); *prendre la parole* (to speak).

Poronkusema (Finnish noun): The distance a reindeer can travel without needing to stop to urinate (typically around 6 miles). Traditionally used as a rough unit of measurement of distances in the countryside.

Poze (Haitian Creole adjective): Relaxed, peaceful; a pleasant feeling of being 'settled in oneself.'

Raxeira (Galician noun): A short space of time during which sun shines on an otherwise rainy day. Also refers to a physical space (e.g. an otherwise shaded space around a house) where the sun is shining, or typically shines.

Resfeber (Swedish noun): A feeling of excitement, anticipation and anxiety before a journey; a rush of emotions or pounding heart before setting off on an adventure.

Sadhu, साधु (Sanskrit noun): A holy person, sage, or ascetic who has renounced the worldly life. A monk or religious devotee who travels around living a simple lifestyle.

Şafak (Turkish noun): Soft glow of first light; daybreak or 'sunglow.'

Se sufre pero se goza (Spanish phrase): To suffer, but enjoy; to experience hardship, and have a good time anyway.

Saṃsāra, संसार *(Sanskrit noun):* Rebirth; Buddhist and Hindu concept of the endless series of birth, death, and rebirth of all beings.

Støvfnug (Danish noun): Speck of dust; dust flakes that appear to 'dance' in sunlight.

Stupa, स्तूप (Sanskrit noun): A dome-shaped monument shrine or sacred site to honor Buddhist saintly figures or local deities. It is a spiritual site for believers to meditate and pray.

Teuchter (Scots): A person who lives in the Highlands of Scotland ('Highlander'); typically used to refer to a Highlander who speaks in a thick accent.

Tikkun olam (Hebrew idiom): Literally translated as 'repair of the world.' Variously used to refer to legislation to protect the disadvantaged; the pursuit of social justice; acts of kindness; personal responsibility to promote one's own welfare, as well as that of the wider society; and effort to improve the character, particularly through prayer.

Timor Lorosa'e (Tetun noun): Literally translated as 'Land of the rising sun.' Name of 'East Timor' or 'Timor Leste' in Tetun, the most widely spoken language in the country.

Tingsha, ཏིང་ཤགས (Tibetan noun): Small cymbals used in prayer and rituals by Tibetan Buddhist practitioners.

Tinogona (Shona adjective): "It is achievable." Connotes belief that all things are possible, even realizing apparently unreasonable, unattainable, and unrealistically ambitious objectives.

Topi, टोपी (Nepali noun): Traditional cloth hat worn by men; forms part of Nepali national dress.

Tu'u-lun (Tetun noun): Help; support; collaboration; joint effort; shared achievement.

Twaweza (Swahili verb): We can make it happen; we can; we are able.

Tzafrir, ‏צפריר:‏ A gently refreshing breeze; light wind; west wind; any calm, soft wind.

Un pont (French noun): Bridge.

Une table (French noun): Table.

Veritas (Latin noun): Truth.

Wee (Scots adjective): Small.

Yanni, يَنعِي (Arabic): Literally translated as 'it means,' used when explaining or clarifying an idea, or as a 'filler word' equivalent to 'like' in English, or 'umm . . . err . . . so . . . ahh . . . you know.'

Acknowledgments

Thank you to everyone who believed in and supported the writing of this book.

Thank you especially to Karin Cordwell, a remarkably wise and generous woman, and Kathy Smith, Terry Jennings, Alejandro Torrealba, Lydia Yadi, Stan Richards, Mary Richards, Naldo Rei, Kevin Greer, Mohammed Sesay, Tom Abate, Kit Turner, James Turner, Ella Turner, Donald Smith, Mirella Yandoli, Alan Miller, Phoebe Lothian, Anna Upward, Katherine Wells, George Robertson, Richard Lawson, Matthew Tuthill, Sheri Miller, Andrew Di Genova, Christine Hohlbaum, Jan Kruse, Arielle Ford, Adrienne Stork, Ryan Scheife, Marly Cornell, and Geoff Affleck.

I have a specific message for each of you—or as Kevin might say (and I prefer), "all a y'all." I'll deliver it in person—perhaps even without a mask in our minty-fresh, post-quarantine world (cartwheels!). For now, here's a message for everyone; for every reader: Thank you so very much for taking the time to share these stories with me.

To write this book, I had to learn how to write in a nontechnical way; a way not permitted by the constraints of UN briefs, reports, and talking points. I had to be willing to write eye-to-eye, heart-to-heart, mind-to-mind, the way we do back home; saying what I really had in my head and my heart, sharing what I knew simply because I'd lived it myself.

This book represents a growth of courage and of craft, and I thank you for giving me the opportunity to explore a new way of communicating, and of living.

I'd love to get to know you, online or at an event, and hear your favorite words and stories in your voice.

We're on our way to a world where all people can speak and be heard about what matters to them, in their own voices and in their own languages, without shame or ridicule or contempt for being different; without control or restriction or prescription of what is the "right" way to communicate. I believe that we're each part of creating that world. And that, as they say in Uganda—*twaweza* (Swahili), "We can make it happen."

We can give that freedom to ourselves, and to each other. And if I can help you do that, it would be an honor.

Thank you for helping me do the same.

Lucy xo

Please connect with me on:
www.lucyturner.org
IG: @iamlucyturner
Twitter: @lucycjturner1
TikTok: @lucyandthewonderwords
LinkedIn: @lucycjturner

Want to be the first to read my writing and hear the news
about my events? Want to share your favorite word,
or chat about language on social media?
www.lucyturner.org

If you've enjoyed this book, please consider leaving a review
using the QR code below. Sharing the good news helps other
word lovers find their latest treasure—and anyone in need of
a multi-lingual mood lift!

About the Author

Lucy Turner is an advocate and activist for peace, justice, and inclusion, with more than a dozen years of experience in international development spanning five continents.

Born in Wales, she began primary school in Scotland, and attended a girls' secondary school in England. She earned a BA (Hons) in Politics and Philosophy at the University of York, and an MA in International Studies and Diplomacy at the University of London, School of Oriental and African Studies (SOAS).

Lucy has led innovative peace-building and development initiatives, underpinned by quality monitoring and evaluation and productive partnerships to support women's justice, governance, and human rights. She is passionate about the role of stories and statistics in enabling united, evidence-based action and development effectiveness.

As a policy specialist at UN headquarters in New York City, Lucy works to find ways for people affected by conflict and poverty to communicate with decision-makers, so people in need can receive the resources and respect they need to flourish. In Liberia, Sierra Leone, Timor Leste, Nepal, Palestine, San Quentin Prison, and now at the United Nations Headquarters, she has seen how enabling people to speak and be heard promotes empowerment, empathy, and measurable improvements in lives and institutions.

After studying the neuroscientific basis for the power of words, Lucy committed to strengthening the international system by helping people to speak and be heard, in their own voices and languages. Lucy's work aims to ensure that the UN hears and helps the world's most vulnerable people. She envisages a UN that is built around their needs, through a process of listening that affirms their humanity and the value of their knowledge.

An award-winning writer and sell-out speaker, Lucy shares words of wisdom from ancient and modern languages and humorous stories from more than fifty countries. She has won the University of York Politics, Philosophy and Economics Prize (2006); the Young Enterprise Award (2002); the David Rattray Memorial Prize (2009); and the Langwith-Scott Award for the Arts (2007). She serves at the United Nations Development Program (UNDP) Crisis Bureau, and on the Harvard University Think Tank on Global Education.

Made in the USA
Monee, IL
14 June 2023